· *L*earn 10 things you can do to turn life into an "adventure"

· *L*augh as you follow the author on amazing travel excursions

· *L*ink your present dreams to your future achievements

· *L*et go of the past and luxuriate in the present

· *L*ocate yourself and the future in a planned legacy

· *L*ive with a new perspective and understanding of yourself

· *L*ove the author's writing style and wonderful sense of humour

· *L*ook forward to her next adventures!

Make every day an adventure!
Linda

What Others Are Saying....

Dr. Hancock is a living example of success through dedication and the willingness to work hard to achieve a dream. This book is just one more example from her life of what is possible for us all. Dr. Hancock shows us that a combination of persistence and grace can work miracles.

—Dr. Paul Jerry, Associate Professor, Athabasca University

Linda has a unique way of teaching life lessons that helped me to change the way I live my life. She uses real life examples and adds her own special blend of humour to keep me laughing and learning at the same time. I love her practical and applicable approach to such an important subject. If you want to start living a better life today, buy this book now!

—Robin Thompson, TRS/MS, Speaker, Trainer, Author, and President of Thompson Training & Keynote, Inc.

Linda has a gift for translating complex concepts into simple language that promotes understanding. She has a global perspective and touches lives at a personal level. In her coursework and as the keynote speaker for convocation, she demonstrated her passion for excellence and desire to improve our world – always with a delightful sense of humour. We are proud of her accomplishments and look forward to hearing about her further adventures.

—Caroll Ryan, PsyD, President and Chief Academic Officer, Southern California University for Professional Studies

I was once a student of yours in the Criminology program and very much enjoyed your classes. I'm not very good with words but, I just wanted to say thanks for presenting psychology in an interesting way. I was never too fond of psychology but the way you present it is enjoyable. I always find myself reading your All Psyched Up articles and enjoy them. Basically I just wanted to let you know you've impacted one person by being you. Thanks!

—Ammy Blenner-Hassett, Assistant Purchaser, Cypress County

…you saw me about seven years ago in high school and were basically the catalyst for me changing my life. I live in Vancouver now and I'm in my first year of getting my Master's degree in Counselling Psychology. I just wanted to let you know

that I still really appreciate the work you did with me...it was truly life changing. I hope to have the same patience, grace, and kindness that you possess in my own work as a counsellor and help adolescents as much as you helped me.

—Kendra

Linda is a professional who supports our community in many ways. She chaired a fundraiser for our local Women's Shelter, donates and volunteers for numerous organizations and helps the media to educate and inform the public on various topics. At a Mayor's Dinner that I hosted she provided the entertainment for my guests through stories and song. Linda is an enthusiastic and loyal citizen who is an excellent ambassador for our city. I wish her the very best as she continues to remind us that "Life is an Adventure".

—Garth Vallely, Former Mayor of Medicine Hat, Alberta, Canada

As her travel agent, it has been a pleasure being a co-conspirator on Linda's many worldly adventures. She can turn any trip into a trip of a lifetime. I so enjoy waiting for Linda to call me upon her return and hear all of her many wonderful stories.

—Candace Paton CTC, Travel Consultant, AMA TRAVEL

Have you ever met someone with whom you felt an instant connection? Then you know Linda! Her ability to enroll her audience with what I call "Higher-consciousness story-telling" is amazing! Full of colour and feeling, her stories come to life in all of us. Her message is presented in such a way as to entertain as much as educate and it will leave you thirsting for more. I truly enjoyed every moment I spent with Linda, as I'm sure you will too...

—Paul B. Arsenault, President, energeia inc. – sustainability solutions
www.energeiainc.com

Thank you for your inspiring message at our 10th Annual Community Health meeting. It was most enjoyable to learn about some of your adventures and your dress is beautiful! Comments received from staff were very positive. You certainly added to our event with your message and humour. It is great to have someone with your talent as part of our Palliser Health "family".

—Janice Blair, Vice-President
Community Health, Palliser Health Region

Also by Dr. Hancock:

Loving Your Life
*Learning from the Past, Living in the Present and
Looking Forward to the Future*

Workplace Bullying

The Sport in Team and Playing the Game

Adventure Series

Divorce: Decision-Making with Dignity

All Psyched Up

For more information view Dr. Hancock's websites:

www.drlindahancock.com
To learn about business services

www.LindaHancockSpeaks.com
To gather information about speaking and writing services

Life is an Adventure
...EVERY STEP OF THE WAY

Life is an Adventure

...EVERY STEP OF THE WAY

10 CITIES

10 STORIES

10 LIFE LESSONS

DR. LINDA HANCOCK

Published by Advantage, Charleston, South Carolina.
Member of Advantage Media Group.

ADVANTAGE is a registered trademark and the Advantage colophon is a trademark of Advantage Media Group, Inc.

Printed in the United States of America.

ISBN: 978-1-59932-041-0
LCCN: 2008934428

Most Advantage Media Group titles are available at special quantity discounts for bulk purchases for sales promotions, premiums, fundraising, and educational use. Special versions or book excerpts can also be created to fit specific needs.

For more information, please write: Special Markets, Advantage Media Group, P.O. Box 272, Charleston, SC 29402 or call 1.866.775.1696.

Graphic design by Rob Walter
www.digitalimpress.ca

Interior Photographs from the family collection of the author

Portrait Photographs of Dr. Hancock by Len Moser Photography
www.moserphoto.com

Editing by Gail Buente editation
editing services
peace of mind through mindful editing
buente@telus.net

This book is dedicated

To those who went before...
My Grandparents
and
My Father and Mother
-who pioneered and set the tone for the family

To those who walk beside...
My many friends and family members
-who love me unconditionally and encourage me to grow

And To those who are yet to come...
All of you
-who will influence me and share new adventures in the future

Acknowledgments

Life is not lived in isolation and this book was not the work of one person. In fact, it is a compilation of the experiences that I have had over my lifetime and the influences of hundreds of individuals.

Over the years I have attended workshops during which I was asked to list my values and received strange looks from others when I claim that in the top five is the group of professionals in my life. I am so thankful for my business assistant, accountant, lawyer, hairstylist, cleaning lady, graphic designer, photographer, massage therapist, doctor, financial planner, insurance expert, travel agent and all the others who help me to be the best I can be because they do all "the hard stuff."

Many friends have graciously listened and continue to listen (for hours and hours on end) as I think out loud. They have encouraged me to think and share my ideas. Thank you Elsie, Chris, Jeannie, Anya, Gail and Linda.

Advantage Media Group has made the process of going from blank paper to published book an organized and interesting adventure. I have appreciated the support of Adam Witty, John Myers and their amazing team in this endeavour. Gail Buente, my copy editor, performed a "polishing act" on the manuscript.

My elder son, Rob Walter serves as my soundman, product developer and computer expert. He makes me look and sound far better than if I were left on my own and I appreciate his commitment to excellence.

My daughter, Kristal Goodman, was my travelling companion in the San Francisco adventure. She also contributed her opinion, which you will enjoy in the Don Ho story, and challenged me to call the FBI after my adventure in Seattle.

Mark Walter is my younger son and I am so thankful for his listening skills. He lets me talk and talk and talk and then, just when I think he has tuned out, he responds with one sentence that is packed full of wisdom and humour.

Many people have dreams but not everyone has someone who can help turn them into reality. I am so thankful to have joint ventured with Tom Antion. He is a man who has a vision for me that is way bigger than one I could have imagined, the skills to lead me step by step towards its realization, and the patience to wait for me until I really "get it." I look forward to each step of the amazing adventure he has planned for me.

Finally, I acknowledge my grandchildren who bring delight to my life and give me reasons to write and sing and play and laugh!

My life truly is an adventure and I am grateful to each of you who has taken steps with me on journeys that have made it richer. I thank you for that and look forward to the next adventure.

Linda

Foreword

It was Wednesday, September 13, 2006 and when my cell phone rang I had no idea that it would be the beginning of a new joint venture. When the female voice asked "Is this Tom Antion?" I replied with "It depends on whether I owe you money or not".

Linda Hancock explained that she was a Registered Psychologist from Alberta Canada who wanted to change her business plan. Because of this she had purchased two older sets of CDs entitled "Mega University for Writers" and "Mega University for Speakers". After filling two binders full of notes she chose me from all the speakers as the person who she believed would help her to develop a passive income.

Using my standard practice of trying to disqualify people, I explained to her that having four degrees and being in university for twenty-two years might not be compatible with the type of mentee program I had set up. She quickly explained that she had only been in university on a part-time basis (which translates to the equivalent of eleven and a half years full-time). That was a relief!

Linda seemed determined to work with me and I told her that the good news was she might be teachable because she had been a student for so many years. Little did I know that this statement just made her even more determined to show me what a good mentee could be.

I explained that she would need to review my materials and that would take four or five months. She did it in five DAYS!

Linda was invited to come to my beautiful Retreat Center in Virginia Beach, Virginia for the November mentee program but was too busy! She was off to Dallas Texas for Zig Zigler's 80th birthday party, but we agreed that she would attend the retreat beginning December 14, 2006.

The limo was at the airport and everyone showed up – except Linda! My staff made efforts to get her flight information and, without success, finally called her sister and office assistant to state that she was "missing". No one knew where she was. She didn't even have a cell phone! It's not that I was so concerned about "her" because it meant we would save some food costs at the retreat hahaha, but up to that point I had never "lost" a mentee and I didn't want to ruin my perfect record.

Finally, several hours later, the doorbell rang and, there she was! Immediately I told her to contact her brother-in-law who had called more than once because of the family's concern for her safety. She looked surprised and asked "Why?"

I said "Because you're missing" and she calmly said "No I'm not. I'm right here."

Apparently the Washington DC airport had been closed due to fog and she had waited for eleven hours to catch a flight. She just never thought she should call anyone because she is used to being independent and she had been having such a good time making friends of all the other stranded passengers.

That night six of us sat at the table and laughed as she told story after story about her "adventures".

Months have passed and I have had a chance to get to know this lady much better. I have found out that she is very intelligent, ambitious and determined to demonstrate excellence in her life. She has a unique combination of respectable credentials and a hilarious sense of humour. Frankly, she makes me laugh!

I have watched her attack concepts that were new to her with gusto. In weeks, she grew from a volunteer giving little speeches to becoming a respected Professional Speaker who attended the National Speakers Association workshop in Denver. She developed a new business model, continued to serve as an Expert Witness in Court and provided psychological services for her clients. At the same time, she wrote the manuscript for this book in three weeks.

The stories you are about to read will bring laughter and tears. They will also cause you to view your own life with new eyes.

This may be your first encounter with Linda but it definitely won't be your last! Watch for her in print, on radio and television, and on stage. She's a rising star!

Tom Antion,
Author of *Click: The Ultimate Guide to Electronic Marketing*
www.antion.com

Table of Contents:

Adventure Defined

ad·ven·ture - Pronunciation [ad-ven-cher] *noun, verb,* -tured, -tur·ing.

—noun

1. an exciting or very unusual experience.

2. participation in exciting undertakings or enterprises: *the spirit of adventure.*

3. a bold, usually risky undertaking; hazardous action of uncertain outcome.

4. a commercial or financial speculation of any kind; venture.

5. *Obsolete.*
   a. peril; danger; risk.
   b. chance; fortune; luck.

—verb *(used with object)*

1. to risk or hazard.

2. to take the chance of; dare.

3. to venture to say or utter: *to adventure an opinion.*

—verb *(used without object)*

1. to take the risk involved

2. to venture; hazard

[Origin: 1200–50; ME *aventure* < AF, OF < VL **adventūra* what must happen, fem. (orig. neut. pl.) of L *adventūrus* fut. participle of *advenīre* to arrive; *ad-* AD- r. *a-* A-[5]. See ADVENT, -URE]

—*Related forms*

ad·ven·ture·ful, *adjective*

Dictionary.com Unabridged (v 1.1)

Based on the Random House Unabridged Dictionary, © *Random House, Inc. 2006.*

American Psychological Association (APA):

adventure. (n.d.). *Dictionary.com Unabridged (v 1.1).* Retrieved March 12, 2007, from Dictionary.com website: http://dictionary.reference.com/browse/adventure

Introduction

I was born into a family of storytellers and therefore have had built-in role-modeling and audiences since I was a small child. Some of my best memories include bedtime stories, tales told by schoolteachers and the yarns shared by friends during casual evenings of laughter and fellowship. As a therapist, I have been able to witness how story telling can help clients grasp concepts that might otherwise be elusive. My grandchildren remind me of the power that stories have in the process of learning. No matter what your age or gender, stories provide a unique way to communicate - and adventure stories seem to capture everyone's interest!

Over the past few years, I have had wonderful opportunities to travel and my experiences have provided me with life lessons which I have shared with others. They have laughed at the hilarious situations that I got myself into and cried at the realization that others in the world need our help and support.

Originally my individual tales of truth were shared with friends and family. Later I incorporated them into presentations and workshops which I gave in exchange for laughter and applause. Eventually I began to speak professionally. I was honoured when requests came from groups and organizations who stated that they were told they just "had to" have me speak at their event. My mind would immediately go to complex concepts that I had studied in university as possible topics for their conventions and meetings. It was a wonderful surprise, however, when the meeting planners specifically stated they wanted me to tell the stories about my trips!

Often, after presentations, audience members told me that they wished a friend, family member or co-worker had been there to hear the tales of adventure. Their words have encouraged me to put them into print and on CD.

The stories that I relate in "Life is an Adventure" are not for any particular culture, age group or gender. They hold ageless and timeless concepts involving self-worth, risk-taking and awareness for global citizens – stories told in fun and thought-provoking ways. Audience members move from giggles to tears as they contemplate the lessons that life holds for anyone who will but listen for them.

I invite you into my world with the shared understanding that for each of us "Life is an Adventure'.

Enjoy!

Linda

Chapter One

LAUGH!

WHAT'S SO FUNNY ABOUT EDUCATION?

I have four university degrees. When people are surprised by this, or ask me if this isn't a little bit excessive, I just tell them, "I don't golf and I needed to put my time and money somewhere!" So I went to school. And went to school and went to school. Who needs to chase a little golf ball around when you can chase after knowledge instead?

When I finished my first degree, everyone was thrilled. My aunt and uncle had a special dinner party and we invited friends and family to celebrate. I received gifts, cards, letters and telephone calls from people who said they were proud of me. My motivation for completing a degree had  been very practical. I wanted to earn a decent living and believed that, as a professional, it was more probable. I knew that only one individual in a hundred had a post-secondary degree, but I believed this would be a good route for me.

My Bachelor of Social Work degree did open doors that I would not otherwise have entered. With it, however, came some disadvantages. One of these, I quickly realized was the fact that I was in an extremely stressful field of work.

I had taken extra credits while studying for my first degree and therefore only needed to complete four classes to earn my second degree - a Bachelor of Arts. This didn't seem to make much sense in that it wouldn't further my career, but I thought it might give me an advantage in future job interviews. This time the convocation ceremony was less well attended by my family. In fact, there wasn't much thrill for anyone, including me. It was more of a formality. Now I had two degrees and was still working in a very stressful field.

I believed I needed a Master's degree in order to change careers and therefore enrolled in an Education program. (Maybe my mother had been right. She thought I should become a teacher.) After one of my classes, a young professor talked with some peers and me about a new program that the University was introducing in the field of Counselling Psychology. By this time, studying had become a comfortable habit so instead of stopping with the twelve required courses for the Master of Education degree, I went on to complete twenty-one courses and earned a "Counselling Psychology Specialization" designation on the parchment.

My family asked "Do we have to go to that ceremony thing again?" I gladly gave them permission to stay home. They seemed relieved!

WHAT'S UP DOC?

My next adventure involved investing two years and a lot of money into the process of becoming registered with the *College of Alberta Psychologists*. The internship and work was interesting but, after a couple of years, I realized how much I missed studying. I tried teaching at the university level but that wasn't what I craved. Finally, I gave in to the temptation to satisfy my learning addiction and enrolled in a Doctoral program.

By the time I finished, my family members didn't know what degree I had, what *summa cum laude* meant or the difference between being a psychologist and being a psychiatrist. They were not even sure what kind of work I would do with my new title and knowledge. I had twenty-two years of higher education! For me it was a way of life but for them it was just a little crazy.

Over the years I had started to notice some changes in my life. I had watched the print on my business cards become smaller and smaller in order to accommodate all the degrees and titles. My secretary threatened to quit typing my letters if I earned any more degrees claiming she was already tired of having to put all the letters behind my name. I began running out of wall space for the parchments. People even started treating me differently and that was a bit uncomfortable. Those much older than me began calling me "Doctor" instead of the usual "Linda." They expected me to have answers to *all* of their problems. My son would leave me voice mail messages that said, "I need a shrink." And the work I was doing began to change me.

I took referrals from lawyers for serious judicial assessment cases. That work began affecting my sleep patterns. My days were often filled with frustration as I endeavoured to determine truth and apply wisdom to chaotic situations. My career expenses increased as I purchased liability insurance, hired staff and developed marketing materials. As a self-employed person, I was faced with getting paid only when I worked. No sick leave, no annual vacation or professional development opportunities. My education was starting to trap me, and with all my degrees, I was still working in a stressful occupation!

SELF-THERAPY

One of my peers suggested that I add "Dr." to the name on my credit card. I was curious about the reasoning behind this. He smiled and said, "It doesn't do anything for anybody, but it does get you good hotel rooms!" His comment made me laugh and I started to realize how much I missed laughing. In fact, because of the demands and seriousness of my work I was missing a lot of things, like writing for fun and telling stories that made people smile. I missed reading paperback fiction, playing cards, baking and taking naps in the middle of the day.

One of the wisest things I started to do was to take a week off every three or four months. Like airplanes lined up on the runway, I had trips planned in advance and this provided me with the healthy anticipation of occasionally getting away from it all. I decided to start making life an adventure again by making choices that would better meet my needs. I allowed myself to begin making more spontaneous decisions as I acknowledged personal dreams and desires.

One of my first major self-care decisions was to sell my townhouse. I moved into a condo with a pool so I could swim at 3 a.m. I travelled to the inner city of Seattle and talked with people about street drugs (just for fun). I rode the city bus in Atlanta after a Memorial Service for Rosa Parks. I took my grandchildren to the Medicine Hat Stampede. I watched classic movies. I drank wine and ate cheesecake! I attended a *National Speakers Association* meeting in Denver. And I started writing this book. Through it all – I laughed.

I made another very important decision. Even though some people thought that I "had it made", I decided that there were some things in life and my career that were just not healthy for me. Even if I was being paid $8 million an hour, I wouldn't do them anymore. I realized that just because you are trained to do something and experienced at it, doesn't mean you *must* do it. At that moment I decided to marry my education and skills with my passions. I started to apply principles that I had taught my clients to my own life. For years, I had promoted the idea that we can do well if we work in our area of skill but work becomes "fun" when are operating in our area of giftedness. I committed to myself that I would work in my area of giftedness in the future. I drew up a new business plan that would include writing, speaking and helping others to reach their potential. Just thinking about the idea made me feel better! And I felt excited to begin!

PERSPECTIVE

Recently my friend, Tom Antion, and I were talking about creating the cover for this book. We were trying to decide how my name would be written on the front cover. Would it be Linda Hancock, Dr. Linda Hancock or Dr. Linda Hancock, BA, BSW, M.Ed., PSY.D.? Tom put it all in perspective when he said, "I think it might scare some people if you put all that EIEIO behind your name! EIEIO would scare a lot of people, especially if they didn't know you." (That's because I am not the "starched shirt" that so many letters might imply.)

I have come to the realization that education needs to be kept in perspective. The process is far greater than merely learning skills. In fact, I believe that the true value of education is found in the self-reflection opportunities that it offers. My degrees have helped me to learn a lot about myself! Education has given me options and opportunities but it has also taught me how to choose what is most important for my well-being. I love to learn and have committed a great deal of my life to that process. At the same time, I realize that I love to share my ideas in a story-telling and humourous manner that results in all of us laughing and learning together.

Research claims that laughter strengthens the immune system, reduces food cravings, provides an internal workout for organs, enhances relationships with others, lowers stress and may even prevent disease.

Laugh every day! Don't take yourself too seriously – even if you are outrageously well educated!

No matter what your calling or mission in life, I encourage you to remember the things that bring you pleasure – and do them! If you find yourself "trapped" in a role or job or habit, think about what you are missing and how you might return to it. Is it a sporting activity, watching the sunset, listening to a favourite song, drawing cartoons, playing board games, talking "nonsense" with friends, gardening or dancing? What is it that makes you laugh?

Sometimes we can't laugh because we are too stressed. Is there something that you need to *stop* doing that will allow you the freedom to laugh? You are the only one who knows deep down what is best for you.

Oh, and don't forget to laugh at yourself. That puts everything in perspective!

LINDA, EIEIO

Remember...

We need to celebrate accomplishments

Education opens doors for us

Sometimes our family and friends aren't as enthused about things as we are

Reaching our goals doesn't always bring a healthy lifestyle

Building a business can be expensive and stressful

We need to have adventures to anticipate

Some things are too costly to continue

It is important to let go of things that drain us

Learning about ourselves is enlightening

To laugh several times a day!

Notes:

_____
_____
_____
_____
_____
_____
_____
_____
_____
_____
_____
_____
_____
_____
_____
_____
_____
_____
_____
_____
_____
_____
_____
_____
_____
_____
_____
_____

Chapter Two

LEAVE THE PAST BEHIND

WE ALL HAVE A HISTORY

In 1852 Katrina Oldsdattr Bokko Uppheim Tokheim stood on the windblown shore of Languen, Norway with her brother-in-law, Jorgen Tokheim and others. Ahead of her, a severe winter storm buffeted the sea where her husband was fishing, and she was afraid. Samson Jorgenson Tokheim, and his company of commercial fishermen had been catching herring. Now the vulnerable ship was visible from shore but was too far out to sea for the onlookers to help. The boat sank and all of the fishermen drowned. Katrina was now a widow. She was 44 years old and left with six children ranging from two to sixteen years of age as well as bitter feelings towards her brother-in-law. She felt he should have at least tried to save his brother.

From that day on, Katrina refused to use the name Tokheim. Instead she took her husband's first name "Samson" as her own. A subsequent generation decided to add a "p" to that spelling. My maternal grandmother's maiden name was therefore "Sampson."

This story, which is over 150 years old, holds within it memories of adventure, associated feelings, relationship problems and generational consequences.

Each of us has a history. Some of it is recorded, some is passed verbally from one person to another, and some it is lost.

MY ADVENTURES IN SEARCHING FOR ROOTS

When I traced the lineage of my parents, I was sometimes surprised at what I found. A trip to a graveyard would reveal previously unknown spellings of names or specific dates of a relative's birth and death. Older relatives who I visited in nursing homes allowed me to view photographs or family Bibles where births, marriages and deaths were recorded. Often I would learn history that was housed only in the memories of these individuals who thankfully were willing to share them with me.

I enjoyed learning about the personalities, habits and values of past generations and viewed some of my ancestors' superstitions as strange, their skills as admirable, and their traits as courageous. Sometimes history provided answers and sometimes it just provoked more questions.

At times I believed that the past provided explanation for present-day situations. For example, the patterns of strong Christian values and musical abilities can be observed throughout the lineage of my ancestors as well as in my children.

At other times, I clearly recognized the past cannot be used as explanation for the present. When I read that my great-great grandmother needed a specially-made casket because she was over 300 pounds, I was relieved that my struggle with weight appeared to be one of genetics rather than personal responsibility. Then I discovered that another one of my great-great grandmothers wore a size two shoe! So much for genetics!

NOT ALL ADVENTURES ARE PLEASANT

From the time I was born, I suffered from car sickness. My parents did everything they could think of to prevent it. They secured a friction strap to the back of the vehicle, directed vents so that air blew into my face and even gave me pills that would cause me to sleep while we were travelling.

During a particular drive in the country, I threw up repeatedly. Previously, one of mother's friends had suggested that if she put a brown paper bag next to the skin above my stomach, I would be fine. It had sounded like a really "hokey" idea but, in desperation, my father drove into the next farmyard. An older man sauntered up to dad's window and greeted him. Apparently my father explained that

I was very ill and asked if the farmer would mind giving him a brown paper bag. After a few moments of thought, the farmer responded, "If she's throwing up, don't you think a <u>plastic</u> bag would be better?" The farmer's reply was so practical that it left my embarrassed father feeling rather sheepish as he quickly provided an explanation for his unusual request!

Over the years, because of my car sickness, I would dread riding in vehicles. I can still remember the humiliation I felt at nine years of age when I was sick in the backseat of a distant relative's car! Sometimes it would help if I sat in the front seat (or so I told my parents) because I could watch the road and therefore maintain some form of equilibrium. Often I would take a pill for motion sickness too soon before departure and my head would end up bobbing as I fought to stay awake until our trip began.

Interestingly, I didn't get sick from other forms of transportation—no matter how much motion was involved. For instance, my father's employment with the Canadian Pacific Railway allowed us free passes to ride the train. Despite the swaying and bumps, I was perfectly fine! I could ride inside a boat at top speed or water ski over high waves without illness. At age fifteen I had my first airplane flight and handled it beautifully.

It is now several decades since my dad asked for the brown paper bag to put on my stomach in hopes of preventing motion sickness. Today I travel by car on a daily basis. I have had as many as eighteen airplane flights in a month. Now I look forward to all my trips and am healthy throughout no matter what form of transportation I use.

SOME THINGS CHANGE OVER TIME – MAYBE

As a therapist, I have heard many individuals reveal fears, memories or problems originating in childhood which continue to affect them in adulthood. Phobias, abuse or biases can be instilled in young minds to the point that they appear to be lifelong truths. Some people outgrow problems from the past or learn to resolve them without negative consequences. Others grow chronologically older but hold onto things that plagued them when they were children.

Many people take on the problems of their parents and make them their own. Fear of animals, bitterness resulting from divorce or anxiety about money can be passed down from one generation to another through parental modeling.

Television can also serve as a catalyst for problems. For instance, children can develop significant fears about tornados, hurricanes or earthquakes even if these weather disturbances are not common to the area in which they live. These vicarious traumatizations can precipitate nightmares and interfere in daily living patterns.

The vivid details of childhood experiences can be stored in our memory and recalled throughout our lives.

When I was a child, we spent most of our summers at a nearby lake. One year a teenager was in a boating accident. Her body wasn't found for several days afterwards. I will never forget the morning that the boats brought her body to shore. I can still, without effort, recall the sights, sounds and feelings as vividly as if that situation is occurring right at this moment.

My mind goes back to dozens of circumstances in childhood that had similarly powerful effects on me. Many of these influenced the choices I made as I aged. Thankfully most have not negatively affected my present situation and, rather than being harmful, actually helped me to learn and mature as an individual.

HOW DOES YOUR PAST AFFECT YOU?

Each of us has hurts and sometimes they involve abuse, addictions, broken relationships, death, trauma or mental illness. Seeking professional help can provide an opportunity to let go of the past so that we can enjoy the present and look forward to the future.

Are there things that happened when you were a child that still affect you and the choices you make today? What things did your mother or father do or say that you have adopted as your own ideas? Are your attitudes towards health, money or politics similar to those of your parents? What messages are you communicating to your children or grandchildren that they might carry through time with them?

The messages of our childhood are just that – messages that a child heard and accepted without questioning. In fact, they may even have been misunderstood at the time and never challenged for their authenticity. You are no longer a child. It is therefore important that you begin to examine your life. You will need to put away all the things that are holding you back from reaching your potential, taking chances or setting and achieving goals.

Now is the time to begin to unravel the past and examine your beliefs and their origins.

Columbus discovered that the earth is round and not flat, despite what his parents and others told him. The Wright brothers stood in the face of negative messages that they had heard and became the pioneers of flight. Modern-day businessman, Bill Gates, used creativity to become one of the wealthiest men on earth. He heard many, many people tell him that what he was thinking didn't make sense but continued to develop his ideas into computer systems that have changed the way we now live and think.

Change begins when people act on their ideas despite history, opposition or discouragement from others.

I believe that our ancestors would be shocked if they knew what has occurred even in the past fifty years!

History is a tapestry that was woven with the threads of circumstance and coloured by the characteristics of our ancestors. The past is important but we must not dwell on it, become overwhelmed by it or let it influence us to the point of imprisoning our lives in outdated ideas or negativity.

Were you ever told that you couldn't do something? Has that held you back? If so, it is time to make different choices for the present and future. Choose to let go of the messages of childhood that prevent you from reaching your potential. Instead, focus on the lessons of valour and decency from the past which will inspire you and help you grow so that your place in history will be more significant than it might otherwise have been.

The past does affect the present and the present, in turn, forms the foundation for the future. It is our thoughts and actions which will link past generations and future generations. We are the link and with this privilege, of course, comes the responsibility to make good choices.

MOVING ON

Remember Katrina, my Norwegian great-grandmother? Something happened to her as time passed. At first she was bitter, angry and rejecting of the family members who did not save her husband from drowning. She changed her surname to "Samson." Then she, her children and other family members including her brother-in-law Jorgen Tokheim, immigrated to the United States where they lived as neighbours in the same county.

After Katrina died, the words "Katrina Tokheim" were carved on her tombstone. She had gone back to the family name! It seems that she had been able to let go of the hurt. Perhaps her move to a new country and to new adventures had allowed this to happen.

Are you able to move on despite your history? I hope so. The present and future can be amazing for those who let go of the hurts and problems of the past.

Remember...

We all have a history

Sometimes the past provides an explanation for the present

Not all past experiences are pleasant

Many people take on the fears and problems
of their parents or ancestors

Our minds can store memories with vivid detail

Some things can change over time

Change occurs when you stand against
accepted messages of the past

We can choose to let go of past hurts

We are the link between the past generation
and the future generation

Our choices allow us to learn from the
past and look forward to the future

Notes:

I would like to know
the history.

Chapter Three

LUXURIATE IN THE MOMENT

IF I CLOSE MY EYES FOR A MOMENT...

I can almost taste the buttermilk pie that I enjoyed in a little tea room in Grapevine, Texas. I can see the fire dancers of the *Polynesian Village* in Hawaii. I feel the smooth surface of the marble statue at the *Lincoln Memorial* in Washington D. C. In a second, I can transport myself back to scenes viewed in *Pageant of the Masters* at Laguna Beach, California or hear the gentle tinkling of piano tunes while having High Tea in the *Empress Hotel* in Victoria, British Columbia. I feel the jolt of a trolley ride in San Francisco, the cool air of a Denver February, and the warm breeze crossing the Pacific Ocean. I can step into the footprints of Bill Gates and Paul Allan that are poured into a Seattle sidewalk or stand on the "X" where the first bullet was fired into President John F. Kennedy near the *Dallas Book Depository*.

I see the purple taro buns served at a Hawaiian Luau, the miniature cars and buildings from a 70⁻ story glass elevator in Atlanta Georgia. I smell the custom-made fragrances in a shop in New Orleans' French Quarter and the hotdogs at the Bigfork *Festival of the Arts* in Montana. I see Mount Rushmore and the mighty Mississippi River and Waterton International Park.

I walk through Old Quebec City, Disneyland and Vancouver's Granville Island. I hear the sounds of a rodeo, small-town parades and Snowbird Airshow planes. I hear music in various styles: jazz and Cajun and blues and classical and gospel. I ride in airplanes, boats, cars, buses, carts, ferris wheels and chair lifts. I smell barbequed ribs, clam chowder and popcorn.

I view a mirror reflection of myself buying a hat, hear a Mexican merchant cajoling me into a sale and see lights flicker in greeting to my cruise ship in the Florida canals. I feel rain on my hair and snow on my tongue and the tingle of mineral waters as they touch my body in the Moose Jaw spa. I hear the laughter of children, feel the warmth of a kiss and experience the reassuring peace that silence can bring.

All I need to do is close my eyes....

FOCUS

I've heard that the hardest thing to do in life is to sustain focus. Many people focus on the past and problems to the point that they become depressed about things they cannot change. Others focus on the future and worry about things that haven't happened. They live with a concept of "What if...?" but "What if...?" seldom happens and they find that time and energy have disappeared while priorities have been neglected. Peace is desired but anxiety surfaces.

The reason that I can close my eyes and re-live memories so clearly is that I live within each moment. My mind is fixed on the present and I drink in all that it offers. When I am with people, they have my total attention. I listen, observe and enjoy.

My goal is that when a person walks away from me they can say, "That was the best part of my day!" If they have had a good time I realize that I also have enjoyed myself.

Life offers times for reflection. Each of us has a role in the past, the present and the future.

History can provide wonderful lessons and nuggets of wisdom but the past should not be our primary focus. I believe it is important to review the past with a goal of enjoying memories and gleaning information that will promote our growth. Worry will never change things that are long gone but, like a trickster, will drain our resources and interfere with healthy living practices.

And the future? It is also important to consider but only with a perspective of planning or goal-setting. Thinking about the future should be focussed on designing your life so it might be better than if it is left only to chance.

BEING VERSUS DOING

Imagine that your life is divided into two parts. One part is *being* and the other is *doing*. *Being* consists of all the states that we experience or desire. We all want to be happy, peaceful, wise, lovable, trusted and worthy. When we feel that we have these states, it is easier to live in the moment and relax with other people.

On the other hand, if we don't experience these and the self-confidence that goes with them, we tend to feel that we are being "bad" or "without value." To make up for the lack, we will then try to *do* more. We work harder and harder hoping to please others and through our efforts become more acceptable.

Workaholics are individuals who try to compensate for their feelings of inferiority by doing more and more in an attempt to earn respect and feel more valuable. Unfortunately, the harder we work at *doing*, the more chance there is of *being* exhausted, irritated or even resentful. And, like a beach ball that is being unsuccessfully held under water, the negative feelings can erupt in tirades that surprise ourselves and confuse others. This reinforces within us the idea that we must not *be* good enough. The cycle continues and a life pattern can result.

Living in the present is a form of *being* comfortable enough with yourself to not be plagued by problems of the past or worried about what hasn't happened yet. It involves allowing yourself to enjoy the moment without guilt or fear or insecurity. The result is that all your energy and focus is available for you to see, taste, smell, feel and hear your surroundings to the fullest and then store the experience in clear memory to be accessed at another time.

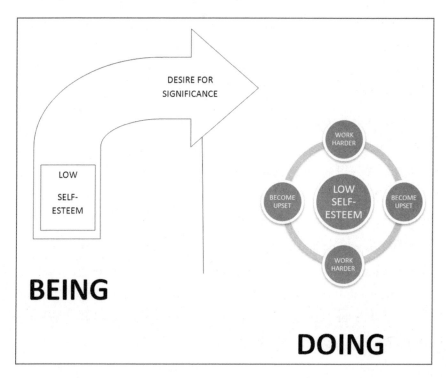

Sometimes we deceive ourselves into trying to *do* more when others actually want us to *be* more. Most children, for example, would prefer to share a cookie with a parent than be neglected while the parent is baking several dozen cookies. Lovers usually prefer intimate moments together over expensive gifts from absent partners. Even employees remember the personal characteristics of their employer more than their performance records. I have never heard an employee state that he or she respected their supervisor because that person could write a business plan in 30 minutes or inspect ten projects in a day. Usually bosses are valued because they are compassionate, forgiving, patient or honest. They are remembered and serve as examples for those who appreciate their personal attributes more than their performance skills.

It is the *being*, not the *doing*, that people treasure.

THINK, DO AND BE

When we are children, time is spent in the *being* mode. We sit under trees and invest in thinking and imagining wonderful things. We experience the freedom of playing all day without schedules, knowing that our curfew is sunset. Our games consist of becoming any character that we wish and accomplishing any feats that we choose to attempt. In one moment we can be the beautiful princess and, in the next, become the fearful dragon.

In my elementary school we had a *Think and Do* book. The lesson of that time was to think first and do later. But our thoughts were unhampered by the discouragement which would accompany maturity and so the naivety of youth allowed us to think grand thoughts.

As an adolescent, I remember lying in a rowboat with the warm sun on my body, the waves gently rocking me as I thought about the big questions of life like, "Who am I?" and "Why am I here?"

Our lives were simple and our schedules open. We had the time and opportunity to think.

Imagine viewing this page if there weren't any margins or spaces between sentences and paragraphs. It would be very difficult to read and unappealing to the eye. "White space" is a visual arts term that refers to the area that is free from type or graphics. When white space is limited, a page can appear busy, cluttered and unattractive. Its presence, however, allows a reader not only to enjoy the aesthetic features of an article but also to be able to read the text more easily.

Before I had completed my first degree, I worked as a typesetter for a newspaper and learned the value of the printed word and of white space. Often the Editor would approach me, stating, "We need a four-inch double column for Page Six". I had the challenge and opportunity of suggesting an article or graphic that might fit in this white space. It was exciting to be allowed a moment for creativity in what was otherwise a very busy and structured job description.

This same concept can apply to life. If we don't have white space in our schedule, everything runs together. There isn't any room for creativity if activity crowds it out. *Being* is sacrificed for *doing*.

When I work, it is with focus and passion, knowing that I have scheduled plenty of white space into my life as a reward and a rest. In fact, seldom can I be caught without airplane tickets or plans for my next adventure. It's not just the break itself but also the anticipation of a break that is important for good mental health.

We need white space in our lives to maintain health, relationships and balance but it will not magically appear on its own. We must deliberately schedule it into our daily, weekly, monthly and yearly calendars. The concept of think and do applies here. *Think* about the value and benefits of white space. *Do* what is necessary to incorporate it into your life and then enjoy the opportunity to *be* whatever you choose to be in the moment.

Remember, white space is as valuable to a life as silence is to peace.

WHITE SPACE ENCOURAGES CREATIVITY

When my children were young, we would purchase new school supplies in the summer. I remember that each year I would open a scribbler and say, "You have a brand new page in a brand new book. You can put anything you want on this page. It is a fresh start." A new year and a new scribbler provided white space for my children.

Over the years, I have had clients who lost perspective in their jobs. They continually added hours to their regular shifts in an effort to keep up with the work or to earn more money. The result was sleep difficulties, anxiety, and other forms of burnout. My recommendation in these situations has been for the individual to develop some white space – an idea that was not always welcomed. They would ask, "How can I take time away from work and keep up, when I can't keep up now by working sixteen hours a day?" Their fatigue and habits had clouded their perception.

Fortunately, those who are willing to get away from their routine quickly begin to understand the benefits of doing so. How amazing it is to see how a two-week holiday out of country can change things! Clients report that they were able to enjoy life through the senses again with the vivid memories of the sights, sounds, smells, tastes and touch that their adventure provided.

I strongly believe that we cannot reach our potential for creativity in life unless we have an adequate amount of white space. White space is about *being* – not *doing*. It is about freeing ourselves from all the activity and demands and interruptions so that we have an opportunity to observe and enjoy our surroundings. Then we are able to focus on the world in a way that will lead to new ideas as well as wonderful memories.

I remember my trip to Hawaii and the demands I was experiencing in my career at the time. As I walked along the beach in Waikiki, the answer to a troubling question came to me. I was thinking "How does Oprah do it all?" and the answer was, "She has staff." Now this may have been an obvious solution to my work problems, but it wasn't obvious to me as long as I was in the whirlwind environment that was demanding more from me than I had to give. My time away allowed the white space in which I could think about things in a more creative manner. I can still feel the sand through my toes as I walked that beach and the relief that accompanied the solution to my dilemma.

Sometimes we don't need more time. Sometimes we just need to be able to use our time differently. Often I hear people state that they are so far behind. They think they need to learn organizational skills or figure out how to work harder. My recommendation is always that they take a break, and then come back with a goal of learning how to work smarter rather than harder.

When you allow white space in your life, you can create new ideas because you have the freedom from regular demands to let your mind create.

IF YOU CLOSE YOUR EYES...

We all need rest, as well as time, for creativity. White space allows this. It provides us with the opportunity to get away from our demanding schedules and focus on the world using all of our senses. In the process we store vivid memories that we can cherish for a lifetime.

Try closing your eyes and thinking about when you sat in silence watching a sunset or savored your favourite dessert or hugged someone you love or listened to a bird sing or smelled a rose. Maybe you need a little white space in your life right this minute. Try sitting under a tree, just to think. No *doing* – just *being*. It's time to luxuriate in the moment!

Now, if you close your eyes….

Remember...

History provides lessons and nuggets of wisdom

The present offers us opportunities to plan and set goals

Low self-esteem can lead to workaholism

Others want to "be" with you

You will be remembered more for your "being"
than your "doing"

White space is important to break up the "doing" in life

We might not be creative when we are too busy

Getting more time might not solve the demands we face

We may need to use our time differently

Being able to focus allows us to luxuriate in the moment!

Notes:

_____

_____

_____

_____

_____

_____

_____

_____

_____

_____

_____

_____

_____

_____

_____

_____

_____

_____

_____

_____

_____

_____

_____

_____

_____

_____

_____

Chapter Four

LOVE YOURSELF! DRESS UP FOR YOU!

AN INVITATION

I was so excited when I got the invitation to my cousin's wedding!

I had always thought we were country bumpkins in comparison to his branch of the family. You see, my mother's sister had married well and her children were also very successful. In fact, one son had done so well in business that he retired at the age of thirty-six years. And now, I was going to his wedding.

My first thought, when I heard about the wedding was "I'm going to have to bump up my wardrobe a notch!" How pleased I was with my purchase of a conservative knee-length burgundy dress with matching short jacket. And the price was right as I bought it at a discount department store!

When the official invitation arrived, it was one of those that had an envelope inside an envelope inside an envelope. My first thought was "I'm going to have to bump up my wardrobe a notch!"

My second dress was a dignified black floor-length gown with small beige geometric shapes. I hoped that with the right jewelry, it would be suitable.

Then I decided to research the wedding venue and was shocked to learn that the *Fairmont Hotel* in San Francisco had just had $96 million in renovations. When I viewed the site on the internet, I thought, "I'm going to have to bump up my wardrobe a notch!"

My third dress was absolutely beautiful. It was an elegant black formal with silver thread woven throughout the bodice and fringe below the waistline. When I put it on, I felt just like a princess. In fact, when I put it on, I walked a little taller and felt a little smarter. Now I needed shoes, an evening bag, jewellery, makeup and a hairstyle to match.

THE WEDDING

I will never forget the feeling I had the day of the wedding. The doors to the elevator opened and I stepped into a world of luxury. It felt like I was entering a soap opera. There was a line-up of waiters holding round trays of food that I couldn't identify. Bouquets of flowers towered over the guests and the scent of their blossoms filled the penthouse dining room. We watched bartenders shake martinis and deposit them into the top of a life-sized ice sculpture, ending their journey properly chilled in crystal goblets. The bride wore  Armani and the groom announced that he had flown the orchestra in from Vancouver. Several stories below our feet the city lights sparkled. We were surrounded by and enjoying what seemed to be the best that life had to offer. It was like a beautiful dream and I was part of it.

I felt wonderful and I knew that I looked beautiful.

My aunt approached me and after glancing up and down she calmly stated, "Linda, you look nice." Nice! I knew that was the understatement of the year. She reached over to touch my dress and rubbed a small piece of the material between her fingers. "You'll get a lot of wear out of this," she said. It was obvious that she didn't know much about southern Alberta or my lifestyle if she thought I would get a lot of wear out of this beautiful dress.

I knew my aunt didn't understand but I decided right then and there that I was not only going to wear the dress but that I was going to try to wear it out. In fact, every time I am asked to speak at an event, I wear my dress. I have worn it for corporate presentations, training workshops and small dinners. There are times that I speak for professional development days in schools and I wear my dress. I'm always the best-dressed person in the room. Sometimes people who were described as "friendly" give me strange looks but I don't care. I just figure that they are likely feeling badly because they are so underdressed.

The lesson that I learned that day in San Francisco is that you don't dress up to impress someone else. Not a guy – or girl – or your in-laws. You need to dress up for you! Because you feel different when you are dressed up and that makes everything just a little more special!

Just walk a little taller and feel a little smarter because you know that you look great.

LIFE IS CHOICES

When I was a little girl I sometimes remember my mother saying that she would wear her "good dress." I was confused. I thought all her dresses were "good". I also remember the times when she said we were going to use the "good dishes" and knew that meant that we were having company. How disappointing when the "good food" was sent to the church and we were left with the broken cookies!

I decided that when I grew up all of my dresses would be "good" ones. I was never going to put the good dishes in the cupboard for months on end so that they could gather dust. When my grandchildren come to visit me – we drink out of crystal and use "good" dishes. They are far more valuable than what might become a broken piece of *Royal Albert* china!

I've also decided that we will eat "good" food. In fact, when I die, if there is an autopsy, I hope they find nothing inside of me but CHEESECAKE!

Years ago, my daughter suggested that I beautify my office. She motivated me by saying "If you are spending more time there every day than anywhere else, don't you think it should be a wonderful place to be?" She was right. I added curtains, plants, a stereo with my favourite CDs and other personal items. The result was a lovely environment for me to enjoy each day. The bonus was that my clients also commented on how much they enjoyed the atmosphere.

You are the artist and your world is the canvas.

Imagine how you might entertain or serve a favourite guest. What type of environment would you prepare for someone special? What impact would it have on you if you treated yourself in the same fashion? Or your family members?

Each of us has the power to create our environment. Life is choices. Make good ones.

START WITH YOU

I am a frequent flyer. In fact, I have had as many as eighteen flights in one month. I find it interesting to watch the flight attendants prepare the passengers with safety instructions before take-off. They show safety cards, demonstrate seatbelt use and explain exit procedures. Finally they tell the passengers, "In the event of an emergency an oxygen mask will fall from the ceiling. Place it on yourself *first* and *then* help the person beside you."

You cannot help another person unless you look after yourself first. When you *be* well – you *do* well. When you look great – you feel great.

If you want your life to be an adventure, you can start today by dressing up for you!

Before you know it you will be walking a little taller and feeling a little smarter!

Remember…

The goal shouldn't be to impress others

What others say to us can result in important decisions

Life is choices

Sometimes people don't "get it"

Often we save things that should be enjoyed

Our families deserve the best

Each of us has the power to create our environment

You cannot help another person unless you look after
yourself first

When you look great – you feel great

Dress up for You!

Notes:

_____

_____

_____

_____

_____

_____

_____

_____

_____

_____

_____

_____

_____

_____

_____

_____

_____

_____

_____

_____

_____

_____

_____

_____

_____

_____

_____

_____

_____

_____

_____

_____

_____

_____

_____

Chapter Five

LISTEN TO YOUR INSTINCTS

THE DEEP SOUTH

I was thrilled to be asked to be a co-presenter with two lawyers for a workshop on "Dealing with Impasse" at the *International Academy of Collaborative Professionals* Forum. Atlanta, Georgia had attracted my attention for some time as I thought it might be an interesting adventure spot. The fact that we would be staying at the second tallest hotel in the Western Hemisphere was intriguing.

Perhaps it would be a good idea for me to arrive a couple of days before the other registrants so that I could view the city and satisfy some of my tourist cravings.

Atlanta is a very large city and the airport matches it! After walking for 45 minutes to get my luggage I was advised to take the train to the baggage claim center. I'm glad that I had asked for directions because I could have been walking all day!

I was the only one with luggage on the MARTA subway and therefore received quite a few stares from the other passengers. Three teenagers decided to become my unofficial travel advisors. I noticed that the individuals seated around us were listening in to our conversation. In fact, at one point, an East Indian gentleman who was sitting behind me tapped me on the shoulder and told me to follow him as this was my stop. He kindly led me to the front door of my hotel as we chatted about possible oppor-  tunities for him to immigrate to Canada. I was again reminded that no matter where you go in the world, there are nice people waiting to meet you.

TYPICAL TOURIST

On my first morning in Georgia, I donned my running shoes and began to lay out an itinerary for my stay. The *Jimmy Carter Presidential Museum*, *CNN* and *Coca Cola* were high on my list of viewing priorities.

By the time I arrived at the *Martin Luther King* complex, I was tired. I was an adolescent when this man fell to an assassin's bullet but the memories of that experience were burned deeply into my mind. It was therefore with fascination and deep heaviness that I viewed the amazing video corridor that chronicled the plight of black Americans during the 1950s and '60s. I wanted to know the details – but at the same time I didn't.

The *King Center* is spread over several blocks. Tours are provid-ed in the house where he was raised and the church where his father preached. Two beautifully constructed buildings situated near his tomb house artifacts of his life and his non-violent stance for social change. The Park Ranger who took us to the King house ended the tour by saying, "If you are interested in hearing excellent gospel music, go to the church tonight as there will be singing."

I love music and thought this would be a wonderful opportunity to hear a concert but it had been a long day. I had purchased two very heavy bags full of books and my thoughts were forming around the idea of returning to the hotel for a bath, room services and a luxurious rest.

On the way to my bus stop, I passed the *Ebenezer Baptist Church* where the concert would be held. How surprised I was to see the street near the old church filling up with television vans, cameras

and what appeared to be reporters. I dragged my shopping bags across the street to a bench that was kitty-corner from the church and began talking with two of the television personnel. They told me they were planning to record what I now discovered was a Memorial Service for Rosa Parks, who had died that week. I could hear the excitement in the voice of one of the men who, in a hushed and reverent tone, stated, "We heard a rumor that Coretta King might even show up!"

When I heard this, I was again transported back to my

youth when I had first heard the story of the Kings and Rosa Parks. In 1955 Rosa was arrested for refusing to give up her seat on the bus to a white person. This action was the spark that ignited the modern Civil Rights Movement and made her family a target for the Ku Klux Klan. She was a humble lady whose simple act of defiance had been an example for others to stand up for their beliefs, not only through words but also through actions. And now, I was on the doorstep of an opportunity to honour Ms. Parks.

Once again I began walking with my heavy load of books. When I arrived at the door to the church, I listened to a conversation that a Park Ranger was having with an older couple. They were being advised to come back in an hour as it was too early for the service and given directions to a place where they could have a cold drink while they waited. I was delighted when the gentleman invited me to join them.

The next four blocks of walking were definitely worth it. This couple was intelligent, kind and interesting. The husband was a retired minister and an author. His wife was a researcher at the University of Minnesota. I felt we had so much in common and was truly thankful for the opportunity to meet and visit together in these unusual circumstances.

WE HAD CHURCH

I believe the three of us were the only Caucasians in *Ebenezer Baptist Church* that night. Together we climbed the historic stairs that would take us to the main sanctuary on the top floor and slid into a pew where we sat side by side. Then we "had church" as the Baptists would term it. The congregation shouted encouragement to each speaker and offered loud "Hallelujahs" with raised arms and soaring spirits. The singing was amazing and would have stirred the soul of even the most hesitant observer.

I wish that I been better prepared and known more about the leaders who spoke in that service before it began. They each offered powerful speeches without any notes and it was obvious that what they talked about was their own history. They had walked beside Rosa Parks in her quest for equality.

Johnnie Carr, a 94-year-old who had been Rosa's friend since school days, relayed the struggle blacks had throughout the two girls' lives.

The Reverend Joseph Lowery, one of the leaders of the Montgomery bus boycott and other protests, had the crowd cheering as he shouted of victories past and those yet to come.

The Honourable Shirley Franklin, who is the first African-American woman to serve as mayor of a major southern city, represented Atlanta and shared values from her heart.

Andrew Jackson Young, Jr., an activist and the United States' first African-American Ambassador to the United Nations, stirred the emotions of everyone in the congregation.

Before the service began, all of these people were merely names in the bulletin. I didn't know who they were until they opened their mouths. I didn't know their roles of the past but I quickly learned from their demonstrated passion and eloquence that they were moving people's hearts and influencing the future. It was history-making in the present.

The service went on and on and on. I was thankful that my schedule was open and no one was expecting me to be anywhere because I wasn't about to leave! The *Philharmonic Choir* provided angelic numbers and led the congregation in the singing of hymns. Finally, at the end of the service, with crossed arms we all joined hands and together sang "We Shall Overcome." What a powerful evening!

HISTORY REPEATS ITSELF

I said farewell to my new friends and once again headed across the street with my shopping purchases. They didn't seem to be so heavy now. I had left behind the fatigue that had hovered earlier. A group of African American women was gathered at the bus stop. One lady seemed surprised that I was there at night and asked, "Aren't you afraid?"

Before I had a chance to answer her, another woman replied, "She's not afraid because she's got a ring of angels around her."

I was the only white person on the bus. The other passengers offered me a place to sit as well as directions back to my hotel. I thought it was ironic that I had just attended a Memorial Service for a black woman who had refused to give up her seat for a white person. Time changes things.

By the time we reached my stop I had new friends and as the bus pulled away I smiled as they waved and shouted good wishes to me.

WHO'S AFRAID?

Downtown Atlanta had become a shelter for many residents of New Orleans who were left homeless because of Hurricane Katrina. I wasn't afraid by the number of people in the streets or the fact that it was late at night. In fact, I was enjoying the walk.

About two blocks from my hotel, a man approached and began walking in stride with me. Instead of a standard greeting he began with, "What are you looking for?" I pointed to my destination in the distance.

He offered to accompany me and I took this opportunity to ask about his life. He told me his name was "Shorty" and he was going through difficult times. He looked after the horses that pulled carriages for the tourists but because of unseasonably cold weather the tourists hadn't been using this service. In a quiet voice he asked, "Could you help me out a bit?" and I replied, "Yes, but not until we get to the hotel." I didn't want to drop my bags on the sidewalk to dig in my purse.

In the light of the front entrance, under the watchful eye of a doorman, I pulled out a five dollar bill but was surprised when I turned to see "Shorty" hiding in the shadows. I reached out my hand and he quickly walked towards me and took the bill with a humble, "Thank you".

The next day and in the weeks that followed, I observed shocked looks from others when I told of these adventures. One of my lawyer friends said, "I can't believe you would walk after dark in downtown Atlanta, Georgia!" He said it with a tone that implied that I had been foolish.

I strongly believe that things happen for a reason. I don't think it was an accident that I had my adventures in Atlanta. Rosa Parks and I were just two innocent women who each took a bus ride but received interesting reactions for doing so. And as for "Shorty", well, I think that was just one more step in the journey that helped to expand my perspective of life.

Remember...

Arriving early allows time for adventure

Asking for directions can save time and energy

No matter where you travel –
there are nice people waiting to greet you

A smile and "hello" can lead to a new friendship

If you listen – you will hear about things you
would have otherwise missed

You don't have to know all the facts to be inspired

Everyone has a story to tell

There is always someone who could use our help

Things happen for a reason

Our perspectives can always be expanded

Notes:

Chapter Six

LEARN TO BE THANKFUL

MY FIRST BIG TRIP ALONE

By the spring of 2001 I was worried. Even though I had been studying for almost two years, I didn't have confidence that I would be able to achieve the seventy percent required to pass my written examination that would lead to registration as a Psychologist. When I heard about a four-day "crash course", I quickly paid my registration fee and booked a flight to Washington state. My desire to save a few dollars on a room and the fact that I didn't know Seattle resulted in a reservation at a hotel that was not near the downtown area – or anything else for that matter.

How surprised I was at check-in to see that I was the only Caucasian in the hotel. The hotel staff was Filipino, the restaurant staff was Thai and all of the guests appeared to be from the Middle East. I was also quite surprised to find that I was in a very small minority of females. In fact, the hotel guests in the lobby were all males who appeared to be in their twenties.

The hotel was located in an industrial district and there wasn't any sign of other tourist or residential buildings. I was really wondering what I had gotten myself into!

The desk clerk was friendly. When I asked about shopping, he advised me that the nearest mall was well beyond walking distance but that the hotel van would take me there the following day. That seemed to be positive.

ADVENTURES IN A VAN

After a lunch of something I couldn't pronounce, I made my way through the kibitzing young men in the lobby. I approached the hotel van that was parked by the front door and was surprised when an attractive young Caucasian woman dressed in uniform approached me. She leaned over in a "let's share a secret" manner and said, "Do you mind if we take some of these yahoos to the airport first? Frankly, we're trying to get rid of them."

My curious mind would not answer without first asking a question. "Who are they and what are they doing here?" The driver rolled her eyes and sarcastically replied, "They say they are pilots." Because I wasn't in a hurry and thought that the ride would allow me a free tour of the area, I readily agreed to the plan and slid into the third of four benches in the van.

It took awhile for the driver to finally round up two men for the trip. If I had been a fearful person, I might have had a great deal of trepidation about the one who entered first and sat directly behind me. He was tall and thin with a very serious-looking face and heavy eyelids. There was absolutely no response to my cheerful greeting. I had the impression that he wasn't interested in enjoying life or interacting with me. This looked like a very unhappy person!

The second man to enter the van was the complete opposite. He was short and round in body structure. He had dark, curly hair and a bushy moustache that topped beautiful white shiny teeth, all of which were smiling at once. His cheeks puffed up and eyes twinkled as he slid into the seat beside me. He immediately put his arm around my shoulders. There was a very strong smell about him that I couldn't identify with any accuracy. As he moved even closer to me so that his body was pressed next to mine, I felt the grip of his hand on my left shoulder. This was going to be interesting!

The driver closed the doors and fastened her seatbelt before putting the vehicle in gear. I looked up in time to meet her eyes in the rear-view mirror. I could tell that she was a little puzzled about the situation.

WHAT HE WANTS AND WHAT I WANT DON'T MATCH

For several years I had worked as a government investigator and because of that, had frequently found myself in difficult or high-risk situations. Perhaps that is why I wasn't as worried as the eyes in the rear-view mirror appeared to be.

The pressure of the man's leg against mine and the look in his eyes gave me a very clear indication of what he was thinking!

My supervisor had taught me that it is best to be calm, but to always try to think faster than the other person. As well, I had been born into a family of talkers and it has never been a problem for me to out-talk anyone. I decided that this was a wonderful time to practice some of the skills I had learned throughout my lifetime.

I began by asking the man where he was from. He decided to make this into a game and told me to guess. Of course, I took my time between answers which included Iran, Iraq and Libya while he would interject comments such as "You're too far south" or "West of that". I knew the names of some countries but had taken my geography classes many years before in a rural area of Canada where we didn't study much beyond North America and the names of the other continents. As a result, I was at a loss about the exact location of the Middle Eastern countries and their proximity to each other. Finally, I gave up on the quiz and was told that he was from Syria. He moved in closer. I talked faster.

Next, I asked his occupation. When he said that the two of them were pilots, I decided it was my turn to make a game out of our conversation. The man laughed when I said, "I don't believe you and so I will set up a quiz to determine if you really are a pilot".

I began with "How many stops did you make between Syria and here?" When he answered "Three," I really didn't have a clue as to whether he was telling the truth but figured that sounded reasonable and gave him the benefit of the doubt.

My next question was, "How many gallons of gas did you use to come here?" He looked surprised and said, "How would I know that?" to which I answered, "Aha, you aren't a pilot! Because if you were, you'd have to file a flight plan and would know how much fuel would be required."

I have no idea why that tickled him so much but a huge laugh resulted, followed by the statement, "You are so funny." The next thing I knew he had his right hand on my knee. Carrying on the chatter, I asked where they were going and got a very vague reply. He said that he wasn't sure but would probably fly around the country to three or four places. That sounded strange to me.

This wasn't going the way I had planned it! When I looked up again, the eyes in the rear-view mirror appeared to be more worried than before. I noticed the strong creases of a frown above them.

HOTEL POLICY

Now the man beside me began telling the driver to pull off the road. At the same time, the driver seemed to be speeding up as she informed him that the hotel policy was for the van to go directly to the airport. My companion's voice got louder as he told her to take an upcoming off-ramp, stating that they needed to buy airplane tickets for their flight.

Immediately I laughed and said, "See that proves you aren't pilots. If you were pilots you wouldn't need tickets. They would be arranged for you already."

A sign by the highway indicated that we had quite a distance to go before we would get to the airport and I knew that I needed to come up with a plan. I decided to try to divert his attention. While looking straight at him, I smiled and said, "I have something for you." The look in his eyes assured me that he would be delighted to accept my offer.

I reached down to the floor area by my feet and grabbed my purse which I placed quite firmly on the hand which he had on my knee. The force was not enough to hurt him but enough to make him move his hand. I then slowly dug through the purse while he watched. When it seemed that I could stall no longer, I pulled out my wallet and removed a loonie – a Canadian one-dollar coin –   from the change purse. "Look at this!" I suggested and was thankful when he took it in his right hand. He began turning it around as he examined the etching on the coin and asked, "What is this?"

I took my time in explaining in great detail the history and significance of the coin.

Well, I was halfway there! Now I reached into the wallet again and pulled out a toonie, the two-dollar equivalent of the loonie. The man removed his arm from around my shoulders to grasp it and again I went through every detail I could possibly remember about the minting of the coin.

We seemed to be travelling much faster now and I admired the tenacity of the driver who responded to my "friend's" protests to pull over or leave the main highway. She firmly repeated, "I am not stopping. We are going to the airport." But the confidence in her voice was not apparent in her eyes!

Well, we made it to the airport and I gladly agreed to let the man keep the two Canadian coins he held in his hands. We all got out of the van and when the two men were out of earshot the driver said, "You did a good job." When I asked if she had been worried, she quickly admitted that she was and followed with, "There was no way we were going to leave the main route." I congratulated her for her determination to meet our common goal.

After I had finished my course and returned home, I told this story many times. It was fun to laugh with family and friends, picturing the man sitting beside me with a coin in each hand, while I chattered incessantly about the workings of the Canadian mint. We roared with laughter imagining how the fellow might come to a realization that he hadn't reached *his* goals. Three dollars was a small price to pay for safety. We realized that I had transformed a frightening experience into an enjoyable adventure.

UNTIL SEPTEMBER 11TH!

Everyone was horrified when airplanes began crashing into the *World Trade Center* in New York and the *Pentagon* in Washington, D.C.

My daughter called me a few days later and reminded me of my August trip to Seattle. At first I didn't catch on but then she started putting the pieces together for me. She said, "Mom, didn't they tell you that they were pilots and you didn't believe them? Didn't they say that they weren't sure where they were going?" I was starting to understand what she was explaining.

She asked "Do you remember what he looked like?" That was not a problem for me, having been so close to him. I have been trained to observe details.

"Don't you think you should contact the FBI and let them know about the information you have?" my daughter asked.

I knew she was right and wondered what <u>my</u> eyes would look like in a rear-view mirror at this moment! It didn't take long to find the number for the FBI because it was everywhere. Newspapers, television and radio were all begging anyone with information that might be connected with the terrorist attack to call them.

This was all very serious. I gave detail after detail of my experience and the agent asked me question after question in a very grave tone. After several minutes, she asked me one last question, "Why did you decide to contact us?"

In a serious voice I replied, "Because I was thinking that I sure wouldn't know how to explain it if you happened to find two Canadian coins with my fingerprints on them at Ground Zero." How surprised I was to hear peals of laughter coming through the phone!

Sometimes life is a strange mix of events and emotions. A high-risk situation in the van had become a funny story. This turned into a serious concern that nevertheless evoked laughter.

I could see the humour in it but, at the same time, realized the high-risk situation from which we had escaped. Often we don't know what we have been saved from until we are safe again! That's when we really learn to be thankful.

Remember...

There is always a way to improve our weaknesses

Our first instincts are usually correct

Life is interesting

Our goals may not be the same as those around us

Skills we have learned in one setting
can be used in another setting

Talking can reduce risk

Danger can force us to think fast

We don't need to know others well to partner with them

Others may have insight about our lives that we need

Often we don't know what we have been saved
from until we are safe again!

Notes:

Chapter Seven

LET GO!
TAKE A CHANCE

ALOHA!

I usually travel alone. This way I can choose exactly what I want to do without anyone trying to influence me or correct my stories as I tell them to others. From the time I was a small child I had wanted to see Hawaii so when I arrived in Honolulu, I was an eager tourist. One of the first things I did was dress up "for me." Then I left the hotel to find some food and excitement.

I had walked for a couple of blocks when I heard beautiful jazz music. I *love* jazz so I kept walking towards the sound. On the sidewalk ahead of me was a sandwich board that read, "*Black Sand playing in Chuck's Cellar.*" I decided immediately to have my dinner in the cellar and descended

down the stairs into the dark club where the hostess agreed to seat me near the group. I was pleasantly surprised to be seated almost within arm's length of the jazz trio.

As I enjoyed my meal of mahi mahi, I allowed the beautiful music to fill my soul. The guitar player was a couple of years older than my son so with a smile, I started to wink at him. When the group took a break, I motioned for him to join me at my table.

SPIRITUALLY CONFUSED

Now, before I go any further, I want to apologize to anyone who is Catholic. You see, the former mayor of my city claims that I have totally misunderstood one of the concepts of the Catholic faith. When I heard about Sins of Omission I quickly latched onto it as a wonderful idea! You see, I thought that it meant you would tell the truth – just not the whole truth.

There I was in *Chuck's Cellar* talking with *Black Sand's* guitar player. My opening was, "You guys are really good. I would like to buy a CD." He smiled. I immediately knew that they hadn't sold many because he didn't even have a pen for autographing.

He asked, "Where are you from and what do you do?"

Now here comes my Sin of Omission. I tried to appear calm and confident as I boldly stated, "I'm a jazz singer from Alberta".

I wasn't lying. I do like to sing jazz – more often for my own pleasure than for others – and I am from Alberta. What I didn't mention was that I earn my living as a Psychologist.

I knew the guitar player was impressed by the way he replied "Cool!" before went off to find a pen. When he returned with the autographed CD he hesitatingly stated, "I wonder if we could ask a favor. Would you do us the honour of singing with us this evening?"

Well…now I had what is known as an ethical dilemma. I had to think quickly and replied, "Well, I'll do one number." I figured that if I agreed to do one number and bombed I wouldn't lose face by leaving the stage.

The next thing I knew, the saxophonist was also at my table. There I was, in a packed club in Hawaii with two great looking guys planning my jazz debut!

ALL OF ME

I have always loved the big band era of the 1940s with the girl singers. I was asked to choose a number and began by suggesting "I Can't Give You Anything but Love." They didn't know it. I tried "Frim Fram Sauce." They didn't know it. On and on I went naming one number after another and was beginning to wonder why they didn't know any of them. Finally I said "All of Me" and they seemed as relieved as I was to finally identify a song we all knew.

When the saxophonist asked, "What key would you like it in?" I nonchalantly replied, "It doesn't matter," as if I was able to sing in any key that was offered. The introduction they gave me was very flattering and I noticed the crowd sitting up in anticipation of the jazz singer who came "all the way from Canada."

Well, I sang "All of Me" and the crowd cheered.

I floated out of *Chuck's Cellar*. I had done a gig in Hawaii! Only when I arrived at street level did I remember that the music was being piped into the streets. But it didn't matter, because I felt wonderful.

As I walked back to my hotel I thought, "I'm just like Don Ho." Then it hit me. I was in Hawaii and Don Ho is from Hawaii. I wondered if I could see him.

THE DON HO SHOW

The next day I went to the Activities Desk at the hotel to make my inquiries. I was told that Don Ho had a Candlelight Dinner Show at the *Beachcomber Waikiki* and I immediately bought a ticket.

On the night of the concert, I dressed up for me and began walking through the *International Market*. I enjoyed visiting with the people waiting in line for the doors to open. They seated me at a table with a couple from Pennsylvania and a couple from New York who was accompanied by their adult son. I was glad that they introduced Don Ho because I wouldn't have recognized him.  He looked very different at age 73 years than he had on television and in pictures which I had viewed across the Pacific when I also was much younger. But when he began playing the Hammond organ and singing in his baritone voice, I was transported back several decades.

How soothing were his island songs sung in the sleepy, intimate voice of "Hawaii's Living Legend" who had years before become famous for his rendition of "Tiny Bubbles."

At one point in the show, Don asked, "Are there any honeymooners here?" and a few stood. Immediately Don exclaimed, "Champagne for them!" I wished that I could have stood. Then he called for people with anniversaries and sent champagne to their tables. Again I sat. Don then went on to ask for audience members with birthdays, those in the military, and nurses to identify themselves. Each one received a glass of champagne. Almost everyone had been standing – but me.

I was starting to feel rather left out when Don's "little buddy" came near the table. I thought that perhaps this man was the stage manager as he had been busy all night walking around the theatre ensuring that things were in order. As he passed our table I reached out and tapped him on the shoulder. When he stopped, I asked, "Does Don do requests?" He smiled. "What would you like to hear?"

Without any thought I blurted out the name of my favourite song "After the Lovin'." A frown appeared on his face and he replied, "I don't know it, but maybe Don does." I quickly said, "It's Engelbert Humperdinck" and then realized my error in asking for this number at a Don Ho show.

The "little buddy" seemed a little annoyed as I began quoting the words to the song. I knew I was losing his interest and therefore quickly added, "Please tell Don that I came all the way from Canada to meet a Polynesian King." The man's face broke out into a broad smile and he replied, "He'll like that!"

I watched him weave through the crowd and place a note on the Hammond organ. Don glanced at it and began playing the chords for "After the Lovin'." I was so eager to hear it and with hopes raised, waited expectantly. However, disappointment set in again when Don suddenly stopped playing, turned to the band and said, "Let's play the song I wrote for my son."

This was becoming an emotional roller coaster!

AFTER THE LOVIN'

Even though I was disappointed, I enjoyed the next hour of music. Then, to my delight, Don announced, "This is the end of the formal part of the show but I always honour all of the requests." He went on to explain that one time a lady had gone to speak to him after the show. She cried as she explained that she and her husband had attended his concert every year to hear their favourite song. That year, however, her husband had died and she had decided to travel to Hawaii one last time to hear the song again. But he hadn't sung it. The lady's story had led Don to a commitment to himself that from then on he would sing every single request that he received during his shows.

How excited I was when he said, "I have one last request and it's for Linda. Are you here, Linda?" Coyly I waved my hand and almost whispered, "I'm here, Don." It was very dark in the dining room and again I heard Don ask for me. "I don't see you. Are you still here, Linda?" By this time I was on my feet and waving my arms. "I'm here, Don!"

There was a fellow on stage with a large search light and he was panning the crowd looking for me. Once again I heard Don speak, "Well she must have gone home already but I'm going to sing it for her anyway."

There are moments in life when you just know that you have to make an immediate decision or live with regret the rest of your days. You have to take a chance! This was one of those moments and so I quickly turned to the couple from New York, handed them my camera and asked, "Will you take some pictures?" Then I began walking towards the stage. I walked slowly because I knew I looked *hot*! (Remember: I had dressed up for me!)

The "little buddy" was waiting for me and held out his hand to help me up the steps. By this time, Don had sung a couple of lines of the song but when he looked across the stage and saw me, he tilted his head upwards, closed his eyes and formed his lips into a pronounced pucker. I walked right across the stage and then I kissed Don Ho – right on the mouth!

(When I returned to Canada, I was excited to tell my daughter what had happened and was shocked when she responded with a loud "Yuck!" I guess we all have different ideas about what we value.)

Don had a bamboo stool beside him and motioned for me to sit. When I began singing along with him, he listened, looked at me, leaned forward and in his deep voice uttered one word into his mic "Microphone." Obediently, the "little buddy" rushed on stage and handed me a microphone.

So, on February 16th Don Ho and I ended his Candlelight Dinner Show with a duet. Afterwards he gave me a gift of his cassette, took pictures with me and said, "Keep singing." I was so excited! I floated out of the *Beachcomber Waikiki*. I had now done two gigs in Hawaii.

Suddenly mood changed. I realized that I was alone and had no one to tell about my experience. There was no one to share my joy with and my footsteps slowed as I walked back through the *International Market* towards my hotel.

BUT GOD IS GOOD

Just as I reached the other side of the pathway through the *International Market* I turned my head to the left. There was the drummer from Black Sand! He was walking very quickly down the street and so I began chasing him. As I ran, I cupped my hands around my mouth and yelled, "Drummer! Drummer!" because I didn't know his name.

He didn't hear me so I tried, "Steve!" That wasn't his name, but I thought I'd try it anyway. I shouted louder, "Drummer!"

He stopped, turned and threw his arms around me when I reached him. With a huge smile he said, "Cousin" for that is what they call everyone in Hawaii. "Where have you been? What have you been doing? I haven't seen you for awhile". This was a surprise to me because I had only met him on Tuesday but I was thrilled with his enthusiasm.

I quickly replied, "I just sang a duet with Don Ho."

The drummer leaned back and quietly said, "No kidding. Not many people can say that. Last night he sang with Willie Nelson." Wow! I was surprised by that, but even more so when he asked, "What are you doing on Monday night? We're bringing in a guitar player from the mainland and maybe you could come and sing with us."

I was touched by the offer and sad to have to reply, "Oh, I'm so sorry. I would love that but I already have another gig on Monday."

I didn't mention that the "gig" was working the evening shift at the Mental Health Clinic back in Alberta.

Life is full of opportunities and sometimes we need to take a chance.

What if I hadn't made the choice that I did when Don Ho called my name? What if I hadn't stood up and walked onto the stage? If I had stayed silent or remained seated I wouldn't have had this wonderful experience or story to share with others. I wouldn't have the pictures or the memories.

DON'S ADVENTURE

For many years Don Ho suffered from heart disease. He researched stem cell treatment on the internet and finding that it was illegal in the United States, decided to go to Thailand for the treatment. He took a chance!

After the procedure, Don stated that he had excellent health and felt better than he had in years. In fact, he felt so good that he married his Executive Producer!

Six months later, on April 14, 2007 Don Ho died.

Several times when I have told this story, people said they thought it was sad that he and his bride had such a short time together. I think they were smart! They had the honeymoon without all the problems that can occur in a marriage! And she has beautiful memories to treasure for the rest of her life.

I walked around in a trance and grieved for two full days after I heard the news of Don's death. Then I gathered all of my Don Ho CDs and put them in my car where I played them for several days as a tribute to him and as a way of dealing with my loss.

WHAT WILL YOU DO?

I took a chance and I was rewarded. Don took a chance and he was rewarded.

If you want your life to be an adventure you need take a chance! And then be prepared for the beautiful memories and stories that will be yours because you did.

Remember...

When you travel alone you have experiences
that wouldn't otherwise happen

We need to follow our passions

It's okay to ask for what we might think are special privileges

Even celebrities need an audience – and encouragement

There are moments in life when you have to
make an immediate decision (or live with regret)

God is good

We are all cousins (Ohana means family)

A short time is better than not being together

Grieving is a natural way to deal with loss

If you want life to be an adventure,
you need to take a chance!

Notes:

Chapter Eight

LEND YOURSELF
TO OTHERS:
WE'RE ALL IN
THIS TOGETHER

JAMAICA, MON

When I was a little girl my aunt and uncle went for a holiday to Jamaica and my aunt bought a lovely hat there. I always thought that I would like to go and see if I could get a hat, too.

After purchasing my ticket and confirming reservations, I filled my luggage with school supplies. I knew that Jamaica is an extremely poor Third World country and therefore rationalized that I could bear gifts and buy clothes once I arrived.

Now, I'm not a conventional tourist who enjoys sitting on the beach drinking margaritas. How delighted I was when the *Air Canada* representative who was an island native, offered to take me to three schools and an orphanage so that I could distribute supplies. It was sad to meet a village school teacher who claimed that she had only had weak tea for breakfast because her salary was only one hundred dollars US a month. The cook at that school told me that she didn't have any problems deciding what to feed the children for lunch because all that was available was rice.

Because I had accompanied clients and served as an Expert Witness in Court throughout my career in Canada, I thought it might be fun to visit a courtroom in Jamaica. I therefore began making inquiries about how this could be arranged but was warned not to leave the resort because of the danger. I was told that there is a murder every thirty minutes in Jamaica. When I heard this, I immediately hired a taxi to take me downtown.

MONTEGO BAY BUREAUCRACY

The *Family Court* building in Montego Bay is very poor compared to Canadian standards. There are cement stairs on the outside of the building that lead to each of the three floors. The bottom floor houses appliances. The second floor appeared to be some sort of storage and the top floor was "everything else" – Justice, Counselling, Child Welfare, Probation and the Courtroom.

In my hand I had my birth certificate and business card. I learned a long time ago that it is important to always carry business cards with me because they will open a lot of doors that would otherwise remain closed. There I stood as the clients in the waiting room stared at me. I was the whitest thing on the floor! A man walked up to me and said

"I like your hair, mon." and I was so surprised that I just smiled and quietly said "Thanks". I believe this was the first time in my life– that I was in a room where I was the only Caucasian. Little did I know that my adventure in Atlanta, Georgia would later offer me a similar experience.

A very tall attractive black woman walked up to me and curtly asked, "What do you want here?" to which I hastily replied, "I'm here to see Mr. Green." When I had been given instructions to say this, I thought this was a code of some kind. I stood by the entrance and a few minutes later, the woman waved for me to come to a room at the end of the very narrow hallway in front of me where she introduced me to a man named Mr. Green. I learned later that he was a department head for *Family Services.*

Mr. Green was an extremely polite gentleman who had a strong British accent. In his small office were two of his staff members. He greeted me with an apology, "I'm sorry to bother you, Ms. Hancock, but I wonder if you would teach us." He then went on to explain that there were only two psychologists in Montego Bay and because they were at the hospital, he and his staff did not have access to them so anything that I could teach to those in the room would be appreciated.

I explained that I was interested in attending court. He stated that the judge had already been advised that I was there and he knew she would want to meet me. In the meantime, I answered Mr. Green's questions. When he asked, "Would you be willing to do a workshop for my people?" I agreed to give one the following day.

How surprised I was at the differences between the closed Family Courtroom I was welcomed into and those where I had served in Alberta. Where I live, the court building features rich woods, fine upholstery and expensive artwork. The judge, who is robed and flanked by numerous staff members, sits on a bench raised nine inches above the floor under a beautiful bronze crest of the province.

The small and humble Montego Bay Courtroom had an old worn table for the judge. There were other tables set in an L-shape for representatives of the various Social Service departments. Each of the individuals in the courtroom had large ledgers where they record-ed the proceedings in their own handwriting. There was no sign of electronic equipment. The walls featured posters promoting health practices such as safe sex. Police officers stood in the doorway, allowing entry to those who were to appear before the judge at the appropriate times. There were no spectators and no gallery for them if there had been any.

I reached into my purse, pulled out a small journal and began recording my observations of the three- and-a-half hours of hearings. I was surprised to realize that issues involving incest, relationship problems, theft, deceit, addictions and child maintenance were the same as those that are addressed in Canadian courtrooms

When the docket was exhausted, I spoke briefly with the Crown Prosecutor who also served as the Court Clerk. Then the judge returned to the Courtroom to speak with me. She said, "What were you writing in my courtroom?" and I quickly replied, "Why everything that you did well." She smiled broadly and invited me to follow her into her office. I was surprised and saddened by the obvious lack of space she had which was similar to the size that we would allot for a school janitor.

Judge Gilloume was gracious and eager to learn. She asked question after question about the cases that I had witnessed and how a psychologist would help the individuals. Then she said, "If I come early tomorrow will you come and teach me?" I agreed.

DAY TWO

The next morning Mr. Green came to the resort to pick me up for the workshop that I was to present. When we arrived at the Courthouse, I again met with the judge and was again impressed with her professionalism and manner.

After my meeting with her, Mr. Green approached me with strong words. He said, "Ms. Hancock, you will hate me." When I assured him that this wouldn't be the case he said, "We have so many crises in the region that I can't bring my people in for a workshop. Shall I return you to the resort?" I was familiar with similar situations in my own career. We were often faced with more crises than staff, so I quickly replied, "Definitely not. I committed the day to you. Now put me to work." At the same time, my heart sank as I realized that Jamaica and Canada shared the same perspective that trouble trumped learning.

The next few hours were wonderful. I met with the senior counsellor and we shared our common concerns about how many needs our clients have and how they might be met. I taught a Social Worker how to do an assessment using a genogram. As I was working with a young boy who had tried to start his mother's house on fire because he was angry with her there was a knock at the door. Again it was Mr. Green who indicated that someone else wanted to meet me. I later found out that she was the Director of Court Services. I was both shocked and honoured.

As I sat in the office of Mrs. Daphne Smith and shared stories of our common experiences in teaching and the similar issues that each of us face on a daily basis in our work, I was again asked, "Would you have a workshop for my people?" You see, the Jamaican people love to learn. I was happy to be asked and said, "Of course, but I have to be back at the hotel by four o'clock. I am singing at High Tea and by the way, do you know the words to the second verse of *Island in the Sun?*"

With pencil poised, I listened while she began the song that Harry Belafonte co-wrote and sang in a 1957 movie of the same name. With pride and confidence she sang about the hard work of her people and the love they have for their country. I wrote feverishly as her deep melodic voice told the tale of her island. Partway through the chorus she stopped to call out, "Mrs. Simpson, won't you come and join us?" And there we were - three women singing together in the *Department of Justice*. Who would have dreamed it?

WE'RE MORE ALIKE THAN DIFFERENT

When it was time for the workshop, there wasn't a board or meeting room so the client waiting area became the classroom. In came the paralegals, the clerks, the counsellors, Mr. Green and Mrs. Smith. The Probation Officers stayed in their offices because they hadn't finished their paperwork. They told me afterwards that it didn't matter because the walls didn't go to the ceiling so they could hear everything that I said anyway. I stood before the group and without preparation or notion of what was expected asked, "What is the topic?"

How shocked I was when Mrs. Smith piped up, "Stress Management."

It was then that the realization came to me that it doesn't matter where in the world we go, things are basically the same. We are expected to do more with less. More work with fewer resources. Like the Olympics it is "higher, faster, stronger" and we all face the stress that goes with that. We are all in this together. There are more needs than hands, more hurt than help and more work than staff.

After the workshop Mr. Green said he would drive me to the resort. On the way he turned to me and addressed me as "Lady Hancock." (I had been elevated from Ms. Hancock to Lady Hancock). He said, "I will always cherish this encounter with you." Without much thought I replied, "That sounds like romance!" and we shared a good laugh.

Mr. Green continued, "My wife is a teacher but she doesn't like to travel. I will be calling you and emailing you! Do not be surprised when I arrive on your doorstep because I have so much to learn from you. And when you return to Jamaica you will stay with my family. We will show you our country and you will eat our food. But do not be worried for we will take you to the resort so you can have your needs met."

ATTITUDE IS EVERYTHING

When I reached the resort, I saw things through different eyes. It was an "all inclusive." I looked around at the wasteful tourists who loaded their plates and then, after only a few bites, pushed them to one side.

I noticed a young girl in uniform who had been working there all week picking up garbage and cleaning up the mess that the tourists left. She always had a smile on her face as she worked. I approached her and asked, "Why are you so happy?"

Her reply was, "Why because there is nothing to be unhappy about today."

Wow! What a message! One that I knew I needed to bring back to North America.

Often we think that there is nothing to be happy about, whereas in Jamaica, in the midst of extreme poverty, this girl indicated that she is happy when there is "nothing to be unhappy about."

My trip to Jamaica made clear to me that no matter where you go in the world there are problems. People argue, get hurt and face personal challenges. No matter how many resources there are, it never seems to be enough to meet the needs of the people or the professionals. We face stress because of the demands and it is therefore important that we support each other.

We are all in this together. No matter what country we live in, the choices we make affect others.

I have decided that I am going to follow the example of the young girl at the resort and choose to be happy in my life. And, I will wait for Mr. Green's visit to Canada with expectation for it will be an opportunity for us to encourage each other.

Remember...

Our luggage can hold gifts for Third World countries

Risk for some can be opportunity for you

Business cards can open doors that might
otherwise be closed

There are different ways to do the same work

People are hungry to learn what we have already learned

No matter where we go, people are under stress

Music is a common denominator for humanity

People are more alike than different

Attitude is everything

We're all in this together!

Notes:

Chapter Nine

LINK TODAY'S DREAMS TO TOMORROW'S ACHIEVEMENTS

SPEAKING THINGS INTO EXISTENCE

Over the past thirty years I have, at times, sent money to Dr. Robert Schuller's *Hour of Power* ministry. In the 1970s I actually visited the location of his *Crystal Cathedral* in Garden Grove, California, just a ten-minute drive from *Disneyland*. So it didn't surprise me when I received yet another plea from him to help fund the last building in a fifty-year construction plan for the property.

I have admired Dr. Schuller's vision and tenacity to do what, to some, might appear to be the impossible. The huge church building, which is completely made of glass, is remarkable in itself. What's even more remarkable is, despite the fact that California has experienced

earthquakes for years, Dr. Schuller still in-
vested in a glass structure near a geographic
fault line. That takes faith!

The planned *International Welcome
Center* intrigued me. I decided to purchase
one of the crystal bricks that would help fund
the project and form a wall in the building.
As usual, Dr. Schuller had more than one
offer as options for contributors. I sent $500
for the brick that would be in the structure and an additional $200 for
a replica brick that I would use as a nameplate for my desk. At the
time, the exchange rate made this considerably more in Canadian dollars, and it was not tax-deductible, so it would be a sizeable investment
for me.

Now came the challenge. Each of the bricks would be inscribed
with the name of the donor. At that time I had completed a Master of
Education degree but also had a deep desire to someday study at the
doctoral level. I hadn't registered for a program, but in faith and bold-
ness, decided to have the bricks engraved with "Dr. Linda Hancock."

Now I had a goal – and accountability. I knew that millions of
people would walk through that building, including my friends and
family members, so I needed to work quickly to live up to the statement that I had just made. Inscribing the bricks with a title that I had
not yet earned was a way of moving my dream from the future into the
present.

For several months I had been casually reading about university
doctoral programs and now I thought it was time to get serious. I decided to continue working and, at the same time, study for my degree
through distance learning. How surprised I was to discover that the

university where I chose to do my doctoral degree was within driving distance of the *Crystal Cathedral!*

For the next two years I worked very hard in my courses through *Southern California University for Professional Studies.* Whenever I was tired or discouraged by working full time and being a full time student, I would think about the brick and re-commit to the task of finishing my degree. I decided that the day would come when I would fly to California to attend my convocation and visit the university in person. I also planned to see "my" brick which had kept me on track for academic success.

THE MISSING BRICK

I was enjoying the beautiful, warm California day and light breeze that swayed palm trees at the *Crystal Cathedral.* As I wandered up the long, wide walkway of the campus I examined exquisite statues which depict Biblical stories that I had learned as a child. The sun bounced off the glass walls of the cathedral and the only thing that broke a peaceful silence was the sound of falling water from the fountains in the courtyard. The cross on top of the *Tower of Hope* rose high into the sky as though it was attempting to touch heaven itself.

There, before me, was the amazing new building – the *International Welcome Center.* An extremely wide entrance truly welcomed me into a room that rose three stories high at the back of which was the wall of bricks – thousands upon thousands of them – stacked the full height of the building.

Of course it was impossible to try to find a specific name without knowing where to begin looking and so I approached the individuals at the Information Desk. They were extremely friendly and it was obvious that they were there to serve others. They asked for my name and entered it into their computer. Then they asked me to repeat the spelling of my surname and as the search continued, their looks of concern deepened by the minute. I explained that I was to graduate the following day and told them how the brick had been a form of inspiration for me to continue in my studies.

The search continued as the volunteer worker spoke with a staff person. The staff person called the main office and the search continued.

We were all relieved when my name was finally found. An embarrassed volunteer explained to me that the ministry had changed computer technology after I had purchased the brick. When data was being transferred to the new system, some of the donors' names were missed. My brick had never been sent for inscription and never made it into the wall at all.

I received a commitment from the workers not only to have my brick engraved and installed but also to have a picture of it sent to my home when it was in place.

I wasn't upset. In fact, I thought it rather funny for two reasons. First of all, the only space left for additional bricks was at eye level and below. That meant that if my grandchildren ever go to see it, they will be able to read and touch it. That's much better than having it three stories up!

Secondly, I realized that dreams and accountability are actually in one's mind. You do not have to put your dreams into concrete – or even glass – to keep you on track. You just need to carve them clearly and deeply into your mind! When you *think* that some dream will come true and *know* exactly what it will look like, you will be able to take the steps necessary to achieve it.

WHAT ARE YOUR DREAMS?

Sometimes people forget how to dream. They become so focused on doing tasks, fulfilling roles and maintaining relationships that they don't even think about what could happen or how they could create the future.

When I work with individuals who are caught in a trap of activity or a fight to overcome present problems, I will frequently ask them about their dreams and goals. Often I sadly discover that they don't have any. Like all things, the ability to dream is a skill that is developed or lost. Use it or lose it!

Sometimes I ask people about the dreams that they had as a child, adolescent or young adult. That's often when I see their faces light up as they tell of plans they had to improve the world through inventions, the arts, science or business. Frequently, they speak of plans to travel in other countries or seek their fortunes in unique ways. They go on to tell me of the things that interfered with those dreams and how disillusionment set in as they slowly relinquished their possibilities.

It is important to go back to those early dreams. Write them down. Begin thinking about the details and creating in your mind a very clear picture of what they would be like as reality. You will never see your dreams germinate unless you first plant seeds and then nurture them.

GROWING CONDITIONS

I was born and raised in a small farming community where everyone understood the rules of sowing and reaping. So many lessons were learned during my childhood years that can be applied to other areas of life.

111

At church we learned about the sower and the seed. In my mind I could imagine a very humble man walking through a plowed field with a cloth bag over his shoulder that held the promise of a crop. He would reach into the bag, grasp a handful of seed, and, with the swing of an arm, broadcast the seed onto the soil.

Ancient scriptures state that some seed falls on hard ground. These seeds represent the dreams that we refuse to believe in because our minds and emotions are hardened to the possibilities.

The scripture goes on to state that some of the seeds that do take root will be choked out by weeds. Weeds are the daily cares of life that little by little take away our energy and time until there isn't anything left to nurture or protect the dream.

Fortunately, some of the seed falls on good soil, takes root and grows. The good soil represents the person who believes in the dream and is committed to its growth. Each of us has experienced opportunities in life to work together in order to nurture someone else's good idea or project. We have witnessed how some people are open and excited about the prospects. Others lose out on reaping the same crop or benefits because they refused to take part due to their fears, poor time management or negative thinking.

THE SEED

The laws of sowing and reaping involve the expectations of a harvest. Farmers know that whatever they have seeded in the spring will bring forth a like harvest in the fall. They know, for example, that planting oat seed will give them a crop of oats – not watermelon. Sowing corn results in a corn crop – not kiwi fruit. Whatever dreams you sow will bring a like crop. Sowing good health practices will result in a strong body whereas carelessness can result in avoidable illness.

Even the words we sow are important. Often I hear people talk about how terrible their lives are and how they expect their situation to continue. Then they are surprised when life gives them exactly what they predicted!

The miracle of sowing involves a multiplication factor. One seed with good conditions will produce multiple plants. The farmer gets back far more than he plants, as does the dreamer.

I remember the first time that I planted pumpkins. I really didn't have a clue about how well they would do and was shocked to have a crop of ninety-nine from a handful of seeds. Even though I was rather proud of the accomplishment, I was somewhat baffled about what to do with so many. That's a lot of pumpkin pies.

If you are planting something that you want, the law of sowing and reaping can be very rewarding. On the other hand, if you are planting bad habits, little lies or negative actions, you might be quite overwhelmed by the harvest.

I remember, as a child, hearing farmers talk about the importance of saving some of the best seed for next year. A successful farmer knows that if you don't save some of the produce you will be out of business next year.

So, too, with life. If you try to do everything at once and not save some of the work and some of the ideas for later, you will be too exhausted to take advantage of the spring planting and fall harvest. You may even damage your health to the point that you are not able to work at all.

COMMITMENT AND FLEXIBILITY

My mother's friend used to tell people, "There is no point in asking a farmer to do anything when he's in the field". Farm families would take the winter to plan and prepare for the two weeks in spring when conditions were best for seeding and the two weeks in fall when the weather and crop maturity meet. Timing is important in life. We need to be able to consider the best times for planning, preparing, planting and harvesting or miss out on the opportunity to do well.

Sowing and harvesting require commitment and excellent timing!

The prairie provinces of Canada used to be known as the "Breadbasket of the World." Our focus was on growing Number One Red Spring Wheat. Over the past few decades, however, other countries have improved their farming practices. To stay competitive, the Canadian prairies have diversified farming operations by growing specialty crops of peas, lentils and herbs as well as breeding animals such as ostrich, llamas and buffalo.

In order to have maximum production of excellent quality, farmers have had to study, experiment and develop networks of support.

Although the principles of life remain the same, planting dreams also requires flexibility, openness to change and commitment to learning.

We need to take care of our crops after they are planted. Spraying for weeds and insects is a regular June activity. Protecting crops from animals may take the form of fencing. Preventing disease is a science all its own.

Dreams also need to be protected from the threats that would steal, destroy or harm them. Be cautious about who you talk with concerning your heart's desires. Find positive individuals whom you can trust not only to honour your dreams but also to help nurture them so they will grow and bear fruit.

GET THE FARM MENTALITY

Farming begins with a dream. First you imagine what you would like the harvest to be like in type and quantity. Then you begin laying out a plan that includes using good seed and good soil to produce the type of crop you desire.

Equipment for planting, protecting and harvesting will need to be secured. You will need to use techniques and methods to enhance the produce, harvest and then store it properly so that rodents or mildew don't destroy it.

Plan, plant, protect, harvest, store, and market. The cycle repeats, year after year after year.

Dreaming is like farming. Whether you are planting a crop for business, relationships, character or legacy, it is important that you are mindful, tenacious and clear about where you are headed.

A story is told about the dedication of the *Epcot Center* in *Disneyworld* Florida. Walt Disney had died before completion of the park but his wife attended the opening ceremony. Someone leaned over and said to her, "It's a shame that Walt isn't here to see this." Without any hesitation Mrs. Disney replied, "Oh, he saw it long before we did."

Your present dreams will be linked to your future achievements only if you begin by envisioning the result before you ever start the project. Maybe you should consider ordering a brick that will be engraved with  a description of your fondest dream! Once you can see the inscription clearly in your mind you will be well on your way to experiencing it as a reality.

Remember...

**Vision and tenacity can result in what might
otherwise appear to be impossible**

We all need goals

Putting things in writing is a form of commitment

Mistakes can turn out to be blessings

Dreams and accountability are really in our minds

Sometimes we need to revive dreams from our past

Farming principles offer lessons for life

Sowing and reaping are natural laws

We need to care for and protect our dreams from threats

Today's dreams can be tomorrow's achievements!

Notes:

Chapter Ten

LIVE YOUR LEGACY
IT'S ALL ABOUT THE FAMILY TREE!

WHAT'S IN A NAME?

T he first legacy that you ever received came to you on the day that your parent(s) named you. And it is likely that each of the names you were given has a special meaning or significance.

Sometimes babies are named after family members, historic figures or celebrities in popular culture. A surname can be that of your father, mother or someone your mother chooses to name on the birth certificate. Names help us to form our identity. They connect us to our relatives, our present situation and may even be carried on into future generations through the giving of first names as well as surnames.

THE NAME GAME

In 1923, Norway passed a law that made the use of a surname mandatory. Until that time, the common practice, especially among farm families, was to identify individuals with a first name of Christian or pre-Christian origin only for the purpose of baptism. In some cases a middle name was added.

There were very strict rules as to how the first name was chosen. The firstborn son was named after his paternal grandfather and the second son named after the maternal grandfather. This rule also applied to female children with the first daughter named after the paternal grandmother and the second daughter being named after the maternal grandmother. When more than two children in the gender arrived, the practice was to begin using first names of great-grandparents, although not in a specific order.

Tracing the genealogy of a Norwegian lineage can be extremely difficult and frustrating for a number of reasons. A Norwegian Christian name of an individual might be found with different spellings in different documents. A baptismal certificate, marriage certificate and Bible entry for the same person may have alternate forms. One woman may be recorded as Anna, Anne, or Ane for example.

Using only first names made everyday life quite confusing and so the Norwegians used a unique system of identifying individuals with what is termed a patronymic. A boy would be identified with the first name of his father followed by "son" while a girl would be identified with the first name of her father followed by "datter." The male child of Jon would therefore be know as Jonson (Jon's son) while his sister would be Jonsdatter (Jon's daughter). This was not a surname but merely a way to distinguish between individuals with the same first name.

Finally, because of repetition and the resulting "naming mess", an additional identifier was utilized. The person's farm location was often added to their first and patronymic names.

Now, as you can imagine, there were significant problems when this system was used and there continue to be difficulties for those who try to understand or chart the lineages.

Let me give an example of some of the problems. My birth name is Linda Roberta Hancock and my sister is Debbie Lee Hancock. If we had been named following the Norwegian system, I would be Isabella (my paternal grandmother) Waynesdatter (Wayne's daughter) Indian Head (the town where I was born). My sister would have been Anna (our maternal grandmother) Waynesdatter (Wayne's daughter) Indian Head. When I moved to my current home, however, my name would have become Isabella Waynesdatter Medicine Hat. Siblings living in different locations would have different identifiers, which would change as often as they moved. How confusing!

It's not just the name that is important but also the process that was used when giving it.

It is important to honour and respect the wishes of other people concerning their names. The highest compliment is to pronounce and spell a person's name correctly and the easiest way to start an interesting conversation is to ask about the meaning and origin of that person's name.

Over the years I have been interested in hearing individuals talk about their names and the naming process that was used. Some claim that they have hated their name throughout life or have negative feelings about what the name implies. My grandmother, for example, was always upset about the fact that her parents had given her the same name as a sibling who had died at the age of two years. She said that she felt she never had a name of her own.

Some individuals complain about the fact that their initials form a word such as R.A.T. or that names such as Abel, Napoleon or Madonna have promoted ridicule from others. On the other hand, I have met people who beam with pride as they tell me the origin of their name and the positive impact it has had on their self-image and life.

Think about each of your names and how you feel about them. How many do you have? Were you named for someone or after someone? Have you changed the spelling or asked to be called by an abbreviated form or alternate name?

The name you were given was your first legacy and the name you give your children is the first legacy they receive. Consider the significance and implications when naming your children. Will the name you choose be appropriate throughout the person's lifetime? Will it bring healthy pride for the individual? Will your son or daughter smile when telling the story of how you chose the name and what it means?

Names are important but each of us is responsible, despite what we are called, to "make a name for ourselves" – based on our values, character and actions. A name is usually given because the parent believes its meaning will be suitable for the recipient. What the individual does in his or her lifetime, however, may affirm or change that meaning.

History connects our names with the acts and deeds that we perform in life. Using this perspective, we actually are living our own legacy through our daily choices. These will be learned, studied and shared by our children and their children for generations to come.

Will they be proud to inherit this legacy and to link their names with yours? What will they say when your name is mentioned?

Adventures do not end with one generation. In fact the adventures of one generation affect the experiences of all those who follow. It is our responsibility to make good choices that will help our descendants. If we don't make an effort, who will?

THE NEXT GENERATION

When I go to visit my grandchildren, I don't stay at their house. They already know the style and benefits of the life they share with their parents and I just want them to know that there are other interesting things to see and do.

I usually reserve a beautiful room overlooking the river and invite the children to stay with me. I teach them how to order room service, phone the desk for pool towels and fill the crystal ice bucket. In the morning the chef makes a specially-ordered omelette for each of us and in the afternoon we swim. I have the children complete the hotel evaluation form and hand it in at check out.

When they ask if they can come to the hotel again, I have an opportunity to explain that if they get a good education and a job they can go there as much as they want without having to depend on grandma to pay. You see, I want them to know that life is about choices. Oh, I realize that some people do well without a good education, but this is the way that I was able to pay the bill.

KNOWING THE DIFFERENCE

One time I had my daughter's son and my son's daughter with me for a "hotel vacation". They were in bed and supposed to be sleeping when my grandson Alexander who was nine years of age, said, "Grandma, I can't sleep because I'm wondering where we are going to go next."

"Where would you like to go?" I queried.

"How about France!" he quickly replied.

I wanted him to know that there are consequences to all our choices in life so I said, "No, we can't go there because you dropped out of French Immersion."

A moment later he asked, "Well, how about England? That's where Queen Elizabeth the Second lives and you like her."

"I think she would be too busy to see us. That's why she has a Governor General as well as Lieutenant Governors in each province to help her," I said and then seized the opportunity to tell him about our history and political structure.

A few minutes later, out of the darkness, came the quiet little voice of six-year-old Janaya who said "Actually I've never been anywhere, so it really wouldn't matter where we go because I wouldn't know the difference."

Out of the mouths of babes...

I want my grandchildren to "know the difference." I want them to know about Don Ho and what a powerful force music can be in one's life. I want them to travel to Hawaii, Jamaica or any of the other 190 countries in the world. I want them to dress up for themselves so they feel good; to know that they need to take a chance. I want them to know that happiness is a choice and they need to live in the moment. Most of all, however, I want them to know that we are all in this together.

We need to support each other as people and as countries while taking responsibility for the next generations. I don't want Janaya to ever again say, "I wouldn't know the difference," and that requires action on my part.

I translate my values into action. There are numerous plaques and awards on my walls that reflect those values. I invest in the things in which I believe. Our College, for example, acknowledges my donation towards the new library. A brick in the wall that was built for our Safe House represents my stand against abuse while my brick at the Crystal Cathedral represents my position regarding spiritual faith. The white queen that I donated to help complete our community's life-size outdoor chess set was carved of teakwood and shipped from Indonesia. It represents my belief that

life, like chess, is strategic. I encourage my clients to learn the game of chess as it teaches us to problem-solve, think ahead and display good sportsmanship.

Being recognized, however, is not the goal. The most important legacies that I believe we can leave for others cannot be seen. They include inspiration for those who are unmotivated, joy for those who are sad, encouragement for those who are seeking, and faith for a better future. We also need to leave memories of laughter and adventure that will remain after we are gone.

WHAT WILL BE YOUR LEGACY?

Legacies come in different forms. Some involve pioneering new lands or countries. Many families take pride in ancestors who were brave enough to immigrate to new places and put down roots for those who followed. Advancements in business, education and politics can be legacies that provide opportunities not only for individual family members but also for countries with large populations.

Perhaps you have a specific talent or skill that you can use to create art, musical compositions or literary works. Would you like to invest in philanthropic projects or causes that help to meet the needs of others? Your legacy might be a journal of memories, a cookbook of family delights or your photo albums (don't forget to label the pictures).

What will people remember you for? Your honesty, the way you helped others or what you created? Will your talents or faith be recognized and influence others? Will your name allow your family to live with healthy pride and respect?

One of the family stories which has been very motivating for me involves my paternal great-grandfather. No matter how much research I did or how many questions I asked, there were only two things that

I could find out about him. He smoked a pipe and was always losing his glasses!

I know that despite the fact that he lived a long life, his legacy is brief and this reminds us that we need to make a deliberate effort to leave symbols that reflect our values or they will be lost.

Every day you are living your legacy through your example and actions. You have the opportunity to make a good name for yourself and your family. What will others remember about you when you are gone? What will you do to ensure that a legacy is in place for those who follow?

The choice is yours – for today and forever!

Remember...

It's all about the family tree

Names provide special meaning, significance and identity

The process for giving names can be
as important as the name

Each of us "makes a name" for ourselves
based on our choices

Adventures do not end with one generation

Action translates values into legacies

We are responsible for passing values to the next generation

Legacies come in different forms

Recognition for philanthropy is not the goal

Every day you are living your legacy through
your example and your actions!

Notes:

none of family
recording history

Epilogue

Each adventure has a beginning, a middle and an end. Mine often overlap or I find myself at the beginning of one, in the middle of another and at the end of yet a third adventure - all at the same time.

One of the reasons why I love my adventures and learn from them is that my tour guide is amazing. You see, my travel companion is the God of the universe and He is so familiar with the places that I go because He made the earth. He drops travel ideas into my mind, helps me plan the excursions and then allows me to have interesting experiences on the journey. When people ask me, "How do you do it all?" I have an easy answer. You can "do it all" when you have a partner who is omnipresent and omniscient.

Over the years I have often wished that I could introduce all of the individuals who I have met on adventures to each other. Wouldn't it be fun to have my hairdresser Tara meet "Shorty" from Atlanta, and Dr. Caroll Ryan from *Southern California University for Professional Studies*? I would truly enjoy introducing Paul Arsenault from New Brunswick, the man I met on a flight to Montreal, to Charlie Harris from NASA who I met on the next flight. If Rev. Ken Luseni could meet Dr. Robert Schuller of the *Crystal Cathedral,* my mentor Elsie, and the Rices from St. Paul, Minnesota who shared the pew at Rosa Park's memorial they would have a lot to talk about.

I would love to watch Oliver Green from Jamaica meet my editor from Vancouver or my publisher from South Carolina. I wonder what the Syrian "pilot" who took my three dollars in Seattle would think of the way that Don Ho took a chance. Tim and Robin Thompson who laughed with me at the NSA Workshop in Denver would laugh at the antics of all my grandchildren who would be chasing each other and hoping that no one would notice and stop their fun.

I would love to take all of these people to the top of the *Fairmont Hotel* in San Francisco and invite former mayor Willie Brown who I met on the wharf when I was there to bring greetings from the city. My travel agent, Candace, would make all the flight arrangements and my millionaire business mentor, Tom Antion would get to pay for it all!

My daughter Kristal would greet the guests. Friends Chris and Jeanie and Gail would be serving a feast of foods from around the world. Paul Jerry, who shares my office, would be pouring the finest of wines for everyone. There would be dancing to Cajun and rock and Christian music and I would sing "After the Lovin".

Zig Zigler would address the crowd and then we would all talk about the meaning of our names and the legacy we have lived. We would honour those who have gone before and enjoy all the other family members and guests who have arrived.

We would try to communicate with the girls from the boutique in Quebec City who only speak French, and Anya, who speaks seven languages, and my son Mark, who seldom speaks but when he does, makes us listen and smile.

My artist, Kelly from Ohio would be drawing caricatures, while photographers Anne-Marie and Len would be taking pictures and my son Rob would be putting live video on the website. My newspaper colleagues from the *Medicine Hat News* and the *Indian Head-Wolseley News* would be preparing the headlines and the people from *Advan-*

tage Media Group would be writing a new book proposal based on this adventure.

Oh, wouldn't it be heavenly! You see, that would be my wish. Someone once told me that heaven is whatever you want it to be. I would want it to be a culmination of all the adventures that I have had and people I have met and loved. My heaven would include jazz and cheesecake and stimulating conversation and lots of laughter.

This scenario may seem far-fetched to some but what I am really doing is planting seeds that will link our present with the future. For we can all be in heaven together – if we choose.

Thousands of years ago God wrote a promise that gives us hope:

"For I know the plans I have for you," declares the LORD,
"plans to prosper you and not to harm you,
plans to give you hope and a future."

—Jeremiah 29:11 New International Version

This book ends with a dream for a future that will not end. You see, my hope is that we will all be together in heaven one day.

Now won't that be the just the very greatest of adventures!

Notes:
Wickham Compound

EPILOGUE

Make Sure You Have Other
Adventure Products

www.**LindaHancockSpeaks**.com

About the Author

Linda Hancock was born and raised in the prairie town of Indian Head, Saskatchewan, Canada. Following high school graduation, she worked in various administrative positions and was an extremely active mother of three children.

Linda earned degrees in Arts, Social Work, Education and Psychology to the Doctoral level. (As she says, she had to spend her time and money on something, because she doesn't golf!)

As a Registered Psychologist and Registered Social Worker, Dr. Hancock helps individuals, groups, organizations and communities to problem-solve and reach their potential. She is a trained mediator who has worked as a Child Welfare Case Manager and Investigator, Mental Health Consultant, and educator teaching in college and university settings. Her professional career has spanned the fields of justice, health and education.

Linda is a communicator. She speaks professionally, serves as a consultant for media personnel, and is also a published writer and newspaper columnist. She has given presentations at annual meetings, fundraising dinners, and community events for professionals, businesses, students and school personnel. She has also prepared and provided workshops for organizations and groups across North America and in Jamaica.

One of Linda's most requested keynote addresses is "Life is an Adventure" in which she combines her personal experiences, extensive work history and academic training into a hilarious but thought-provoking message. Its popularity has led to this book and other resources with the same title.

Throughout the years Linda has served as a volunteer on several local, provincial and national committees and boards. Linda is also a musician who treasures every moment that she can be with her grandchildren.

Philosophy

to live
and learn
and love
in a manner that will lead to personal growth
and enhance the lives
of others.

My goal
is to encourage
individuals, groups, organizations,
and communities
to reach their potential!

Notes: